DANGEROUS
LIVES
The experiences of
(South) Asian women &
children in the aftermath
of domestic violence

LORRAINE L. RICHARDSON

ISBN:1533674221
ISBN-13:978-1533674227

DEDICATION

For my children –
Lolly, Donna Louise & Edward

CONTENTS

ACKNOWLEDGMENTS

I would like to thank Dr. Eric Hirsch (Brunel University, London, England) for his supervision and guidance and for keeping me focused throughout this study. Kal Bansal for her interpreting assistance and her cultural insights which proved invaluable. The study, was an education for both of us, despite our cultural awareness. To my children – Lolly, for the selfless use of her room (whilst she was away) to accommodate my growing number of books and other paraphernalia, Edward, for giving me the space and time to study and Donna Louise, who patiently listened to my ideas and plans over and over again and most importantly, took over a number of parental duties, enabling me to complete the study. I am indebted to the Primary Care Trust who financed my study and my work colleagues who encouraged and supported me throughout. Additionally, I am obliged to the staff at the (South) Asian Women's Refuge who welcomed my intrusion and questions, in particular to Gulshan and Zarina for their perception into refuge organization and facilities and finally, I am immensely grateful to all the women and children for sharing their experiences with me, with candour and veracity. I am acutely aware of the difficulties and dangers this may have presented and I am greatly honoured and humbled to be allowed to journey with them into their past.

CHAPTER 1
INTRODUCTION

Throughout the world violence against women is still very much a hidden problem and is underestimated everywhere. In Africa, Asia Europe and the U.S.A. the problem has been recognized and raised and put into the political agenda, at local and national level. In addition, women's refuges have been set up and there has been an increase in counselling and development of services in education, health and welfare. Women and children experiencing domestic Violence are encouraged to verbalize about the abuse and feminists have been successful in establishing that violence against women is a violation of human rights(Davis, 1994). Despite this the violence persists and forms of violence may vary form one culture and society to another.

Anthropology has always strived to account for the social and cultural variations in the world and part of anthropology is to conceptualize and understand similarities between social systems and human relationships (Eriksen, T.H. 1995). Rather than viewed as a pathology, the phenomena of 'domestic violence' in this study is seen from a specific social perspective, that of the traditional (South)Asian woman and child.

Women are seen in many societies as being closer to nature than men, who are considered more 'cultivated'. Inspired by Levi-Strauss's structuralism, Sherry Ortner (1974) notes, women represent danger to men, because they are regarded as undomesticated, wild and difficult to control. Women are seen as passive and men as active, a view that is generally held with regard to 'the sexual act, the transmission of culture or the respective roles of the genders in the upholding of society' (Eriksen, T.H. 1995).

Gender inequalities beginning with biological differences between men and women and women's links with children, who are considered 'imperfectly cultured', gives women the connection to being close to nature. However,

Ortner's distinction between nature and culture, drawn from Levi-Strauss, may not be a universal model and remains controversial. For the purposes of this study, an application of this train of thought would be useful to aid interpretation of the ethnographic material.

The study focuses on a small group of (South)Asian women and their children (I have used South '**Asian**' in this study to refer to people from India and Pakistan, and the term '**Black**' as a political term for people who suffer from racism and powerlessness, also **British Asian,** a British person of South Asian descent). It is a journey into the complex phenomena of 'experience', - the experiences of the women and children. The painful accounts are revisited through the perspectives of the abused, against the background of cultural values and family obligations. Imam (1994) describes the impact of domestic violence as twofold: the aspect of the abuse experience unique to (South) Asian (and Black) children both inside and outside the home. She notes that it is the everyday reality of living in a racist society, compounded by the violation of their security within the home that creates a situation of multiple oppression for these children.

Unusually, in the study, the issue of racism did not arise, which does not mean that it does not occur, as previous research indicates otherwise. Focus is directed on the women's accounts of their marriage and the violence within it, the refuge and the children's experiences through their mother's voices.

For all of them, it is the first time they were able to speak candidly about their lives within an abusive household and their fears for themselves and for their children. Finally, this cathartic ethnography ends with the women's hopes for new beginnings, free from oppression.

THE STUDY

Generally, anthropological fieldwork involves a long period of time among members of a society, in order for the ethnographer to gain a wide view of that society and a well-rounded insight into their lives. This study was conducted over a period of three months; that is, interviews were obtained over that period of time. However, I had worked with the women in the refuge intensively for eight months prior to the commencement of the study. During the study I made numerous observations in order to know a great deal of the women and children's way of life and their organization within the refuge, developing strong bonds and trustworthy relationships, essential for sensitive research.

The refuge in the study is a specific refuge for (South) Asian women and their children. For confidential purposes it cannot be identified. It is in an area on the outskirts of London which has a high (South) Asian population, the majority of which originate from Pakistan. All the women in the study were born in Pakistan or India; the children were born in Britain, India and Pakistan. Apart from one woman who spoke a little English, it was not spoken by any of the other women in the study. The women preferred to communicate in Punjabi, Urdu or Hindi. One woman who spoke some English was educated to a degree level and originated from the city, the other women were not in receipt of a high level of education and originated from the rural areas of their countries of origin.

I am of Anglo-Indian origin and my early years were spent in Bombay (now Mumbai). Consequently, I can speak and understand Hindi and have a good knowledge of (South) Asian communities and culture. At the time of the study (2002) I was a practicing Health Visitor in the study area and the health professional overseeing the refuge. The interpreting service was provided by Kal Bansal, at the time, a nursery nurse who is South Asian (Sikh) born in Kenya. She assisted me at the refuge prior to and during the study.

The study was carried out more than a decade ago when I was a MSc student in Social Anthropology at Brunel University in Uxbridge, England, U.K.. I have revised some of the original manuscript due to recent legislation on the issues of domestic violence and forced marriages and added an Epilogue chapter with the ongoing legal situation, the women and children's current circumstances after leaving the refuge and the demise of the refuge in the study. However, I have restrained from making too many revisions and admit it is not up-to-date on the recent research done on this vast topic. However, what remains are the voices of the women interviewed and their experiences of this devastating phenomena., which was the whole purpose of the study.

Aims and Objectives

My original aims and objectives were to study the refuge experiences of the women and children and to gain some insight into coping strategies employed by them. However, the women voiced that they had stories to tell; they wished to talk about their lives within their marriages. Most of them were sufficiently recovered and were not in danger of regression, in fact many found the experience cathartic. Many had spent years in silent struggle (I do not want to portray them as passive, but rather as women who possessed the inner strength that necessitates endurance).

By changing the direction of the study aims, I hoped to gain insight into the lived experiences of these women and children, portraying the phenomena of domestic violence from a traditional as opposed to a British born, (South) Asian woman and children's perspective. The children's experiences are portrayed through their mother's accounts.

The refuge experiences of the women and children would further serve to reflect on the needs and issues that pertain to them as it is only through their voices can they be heard.

This in turn will hopefully raise awareness of the multiple difficulties faced by (South) Asian women and children and would lead on to inform and advise current service provision and the multi-disciplinary professionals to the sensitive needs of this group of women.

Previous Studies

Examination of the literature has revealed an abundance of studies on domestic violence and its impact on children. The research indicates that children in the context of domestic violence are more likely to be at risk of physical, sexual and /or emotional abuse, making it apparent that domestic violence is an indicator of a risk of harm to children.

The literature on Black and (South) Asian experiences of domestic violence have been sparse. I have drawn partly on the following three author's studies; U.K. Imam, A. Mama and K. Bhatti-Sinclair. All had their own particular areas of focus but nevertheless all aim to raise awareness of the multiple oppression faced by Black and (South) Asian women and children experiencing domestic violence.

Imam (1994) explored specific issues affecting (South) Asian children living with domestic violence and suggests that it needs to be understood against the wider, universal issues of domestic violence. She recognizes that male power and dominance exists in many societies, but their expression differs according to religions and cultures. She found that due to cultural and religious expectations, mothers may sometimes leave behind their daughters when they seek refuge, to save them from being ostracized by community and family.

Mama (1989) cites, that for (South) Asian women the violence in the home is compounded by societal racism and state oppression. She refers to several cases where the power of the State is used by men to coerce women to stay with them, not to contact the police or have men (the abusers) excluded from the home using immigration legislation as a deterrent, with many women preferring to return to the abuser to escape racism towards them and their children.

Bhatti-Sinclair (1994), focused on (South) Asian women's perceptions of themselves, their families, their relationships with men and the violence they experienced. She positioned their oppression against a background of structural disadvantages, i.e., housing, public services and religious barriers and found that few of the women in her study approached any outside agency for help in the early years of suffering. Many felt that they were ill equipped to deal with life outside their family homes and missed the support provided by immediate and extended families.

Although it is known that domestic violence occurs across all classes, it is unknown whether it has a similar impact on children living in different circumstances, or if other factors have an effect, like the length of time children live with domestic violence, their coping strategies and ethnicity.

I originally aimed to observe the adjustment strategies and coping mechanisms employed by the women and children, but I was unable to make any progress. Very little research in the U.K. has been done in this area. Studies in the U.S. that attempted to measure this factor (Stagg, Wills and Howell 1989; Westra and Martin 1981) both found that white children had more externalizing (acting out) and internalizing (withdrawn and depressed) behavioural difficulties than African-American children.

Both Mama (1989) and Imam (1994) report that culture and religion is sometimes used by men universally to subjugate and dominate women. (South) Asian men too use religion to justify abuse of women. Although none of the religions sanction violence, parts of the religious books have been manipulated making it easier to condone abuse. Imam cites that Hinduism has: '....*strong and ancient traditions of subservience and obedience to men....whilst in Sikhism there exist more liberal attitudes, with some moves to promote equality for women'*.

Ahmed (1992) found Islam has clearly defined gender roles that maintain the legal, social and institutional subordination of women.

All the women in the study belong to the three religions mentioned above. Apart from the baby of the Hindu woman, the rest of the children had all witnessed the violence against their mothers. Research studies suggest that age has an influence in terms of the ways that children are able to make sense of their experiences and this determines the expression of distress or anxiety. However, this measurement is complex and there is much more to learn. Hugh's study (1988) suggested pre-school children displayed more behavioural problems than school-aged children. According to the study of children in refuges, (Hague, Kelly, Malos and Mullender 1996) younger children generally displayed more behavioural difficulties but were more resilient than the older children who understood more, were more angry and found trusting others problematic.

Bowstead, Lall and Rashid (1995) discuss other effects that Black and (South) Asian children are likely to experience. Some children could be subjected to the additional threat of abduction abroad and may be asked inappropriately to act as an interpreter if their mother's first language is not English. This is unsuitable in situations of domestic violence, because it restricts the amount of information the mother feels able to disclose in front of the child or forces them to reveal details which they had protected their child from knowing, raising issues of confidentiality and increasing distress and responsibility for the child. Some of the women in my study sample agreed that they had to resort to some of these ways of communication.

Methodology

Initially, this study aimed to learn about the strategies and coping skills adopted by a particular ethnic group of women and children following trauma and within a specific context. An interview pilot study revealed that the participant's requirements veered towards a narrative preference. In other words, the women had stories to tell. Rather than view this as a technical problem, I realized that it was in itself a source of qualitative data and proceeded to amend my approach.

The Sample

The sample was obtained from the women's refuge. The refuge was specifically for (South) Asian women and children. The women and children in the study all originated from India and Pakistan. None were fluent English speakers. Languages spoken were Urdu, Punjabi and Hindi. The women were a mixture of Muslim, Sikh and Hindu religions. All the women had arranged marriages and were born outside the U.K. The children's ages ranged from 4 months to 8 years and were a mixture of girls and boys.

As the allocated health visitor of the refuge, I took care of the health needs of the women and children. I had been working for eight months at the refuge prior to the commencement of the study. Kal, the nursery nurse who assisted with interpreting, had a longer working period with the women and children and was well known to all the participants.

The study took place at the refuge in the summer of 2002 over a period of 12 weeks. The refuge can accommodate up to ten women, depending on the number of their children (four children would require two bedrooms). At the time of the study (June 2002) there were nine women. One single woman and eight women with children. Two women declined from participating and the seventh woman was chosen from the nearby homeless hostel. She was a former resident of the refuge and was originally chosen for this study but had breached the confidentiality rule by inviting her friends from outside into the refuge. It was decided to include her and her daughter, as both had been a crucial part of the refuge at the conception stage of the study. Additionally, it was thought that it would be important to offer an alternative perspective to the study highlighting the fundamental issue of confidentiality.

The Research Design

The research used two methods:
  a) Participant observations
  b) Semi-structured interviews

It was thought that the social phenomena in the form of language, cultural meanings and social interaction would be obtained by the participant observation method (the preferred method for anthropologists 'in the field'). This was especially suitable when observing the children, who would be distracted by any tape recordings. Data was documented in the form of field notes.

Semi-structured interviews would be used with the women only. This would give them the opportunity to relate their accounts of the events and would be a cathartic journey for them. The interviews were conducted privately, usually in the women's room with the interpreter and myself present, using a tape recorder to aid recall. On some occasions the children were present in the room.

In addition two children participated in play therapy – a dolls house was shown to the child and they were asked to arrange the furniture and 'people' appropriately in the house. They were then asked to draw various scenarios using papers and pencils. The results of this was not successful, due to the need for specific requirements that this type of therapy requires and was found to be beyond the scope of this study.

An interview with the refuge staff elicited vital information on the provision and the admission criteria of the refuge. This was important to note as refuges throughout the country will differ from each other. It is also particularly appropriate to reveal what life in the refuge entailed and the role it played in the lives of the women and children.

Sources of information

There has been an absence of research into the experiences of (South) Asian women and children following domestic violence. The few previous studies in this area all focused on specific issues effecting Black and (South) Asian women in Britain.

In all, the main sources of information were obtained from the literature searches and the interviews with the women and the refuge staff. Additional conversations with Muslim and Sikh colleagues at work helped to increase knowledge and first hand contacts with clients from both the Sikh and Muslim communities with a history of domestic violence themselves illuminated the extent and nature of this phenomena.

The Interviews

The interviews were designed and developed by myself. A pilot study on two participants were tested out in the preliminary stages of the research, in order to test the interview schedule and to perfect the interview technique. Following this some amendments were made to the interview questions and some questions were repositioned in the sequence.

The interview covered the following areas of experience:

- The women's background, their ages, their own families
- Meeting their husbands
- The marriage
- The violence
- The involvement of the children in the violence
- The decisive factor for leaving
- The women and children's feelings about the events
- Living in the refuge
- The women's advice to someone else suffering domestic violence
- The women's hopes for theirs and their children's future

The style of the interview was important because of the emotive content of the material. On several occasions the tape was stopped when the woman being interviewed became emotional. On other occasions children were present, so certain questions were avoided at that time. All the women admitted it was good to talk and reflect on their past lives.

The data obtained was stored appropriately and securely and the women in the study were reassured of confidentiality. Their anonymity was assured, pseudonyms were used throughout and the location of the refuge was unidentifiable. Informed consent was obtained from all who participated including the children who were old enough to understand. All were given sufficient time to consider their decision to participate. The outline of the research was discussed in their own language and all the women received a copy of the details of the study.

Problems

There were significant problems with all the women's comprehension of the following questions in the interview questionnaire.

- **15) Following the violence do you think you have changed as a person, if so, how?**

The women agreed that they had changed but had problems explaining the change. Eventually one woman said she would stand up to her husband and would not put up with the violence again. Another said she would never marry again. Yet another explains that she now has a lovely life and would not want to change it.

- *16) How did you cope during the violence? What strategies did you use, what kept you going?*

The women found this puzzling. "…you just did", when asked how they coped. The answers or non-answers were unexpected. All emphasized that they remained enduring the violence because of the children or feared losing the children if they left. None suggested any overt or covert coping strategies. It may be that the women's belief is that to be a good wife is to endure all, keeping quiet, because of the shame and social and cultural stigma and repercussions attached to domestic violence. Also, imperative is to protect the abuser, for fear of being blamed by others and losing honour and standing in their community and families. So, it may seem that the strategies developed by the women to prevent disclosure were not recognized by them as such, but nevertheless were present

- *17) As a survivor of domestic violence, how would you advise a woman who finds herself in a similar situation?*

Many of the women found it difficult to put themselves in another person's shoes, psychologists call this concept – 'theory of mind'. Why did every woman interviewed find the concept perplexing? Do other non-Western cultures have similar constraints? These were questions that did arise from the interviews and was one of the reasons for retaining the question in the interview. The other reason for the difficulty was, the equivalent version of the question in their language. Does it translate exactly?
Some of the women did not feel it was appropriate to give advice to another woman but eventually admitted they would tell the woman to leave.

CHAPTER 2
DRAMATIS PERSONAE

A total of seven women were interviewed. Six were interviewed in the refuge and one who was living in a nearby homeless hostel and who was formerly a resident of the refuge, was seen and interviewed in her room. An interview was also conducted with the staff of the refuge, who detailed the admission and assessment procedure for me.

There was a total of seven children but only two agreed to participate in the play sequence. The majority of the children (five) were of pre-school age (one was a baby) and two were younger school-aged children.

1 - NINA

Nina was born in a rural district in Pakistan. She is 33 years old. She came to England in 1990 after getting married in Pakistan. Although it was an arranged marriage, she did see her husband prior to the marriage. Nina's husband is her first cousin who was born and raised in England. Her husband's family comprised of five sisters, one brother and her husband's parents. They all lived together in a four bedroom house in a city in the north of England. Nina was married for eleven years and has three children, two older sons (who remained with their father) and a four year old daughter, who is currently with her in the refuge. All three children were born in England. Nina has never worked outside the family home. She and her husband are Muslim. Nina has lived at the refuge for four months.

2 – PREEYA

Preeya was born in a rural district in Punjab, India. She is 26 years old and came to England in 1995 after getting married in India. The marriage was arranged a few days after she met her husband, she is not related to him. Both Preeya and her husband are Sikh. Preeya's husband was married before, but Preeya was not told this until after the marriage. Her husband was born and raised in England. Preeya's daughter was born in India. Mother and baby came over together when the baby was seven months old. The couple lived in a house with the husband's parents and his brother and his wife (her sister-in-law). The marriage lasted five years. Preeya had a job in a local factory, where she would work long hours. Preeya has lived in the refuge for two years.

3 – SEEMA

Seema was born in a rural district of Punjab, India. She is 27 years old. She had an arranged marriage in India and saw her husband a few times before that. She came to England in 1994. Both Seema and her husband are Sikh, they are not related to each other. Seema's husband was born and raised in England and was previously married. Seema only learnt of this by accident, after her marriage. Soon after the birth of Seema's baby in India, her husband (who had returned to England after the marriage, Seema had to wait for her visa) returned to India and after a few months brought the three month old baby with him to England. Seema eventually joined them two months later, and the three of them lived in a house on their own. They were married for six years. During that time Seema worked in catering and cleaning, then got promoted to a cashier. Seema has lived at the refuge for two years.

4 – SUNITA

Sunita was born in a rural district in Gujarat, West India. She is 25 years old. Her father was a jeweller. She was previously married in India. She applied to a marriage bureau and met her current husband. Four days later they were married. Both Sunita and her husband are Gujarati Hindus. Sunita's husband was born and raised in England and has been married before and had children. Sunita was aware of this but was told that he had no contact with them. However, he did see them quite frequently. Sunita came to England in April 2001. She lived in a house with her mother and father-in-law. She got pregnant in May 2001. She left her husband's house in January 2002, when she was eight months pregnant, taking residence in the refuge. She gave birth to a baby boy in February 2002. She was married for one year and five months. She has been at the refuge for five months.

5 – NEELAM

Neelam was born in a rural district in Pakistan. She is 23 years old. She had an arranged marriage in Pakistan to her first cousin. The marriage was arranged by both parents when they were very young, so she knew they would marry when they grew up. Her husband was born and raised in England. Neelam came to England in 1997. She stayed with her husband's parents for two years before the couple got their own council house. She has a four year old son who was born in England. She did not work outside the home. Both Neelam and are husband are Muslim. She was married for six years. Neelam and her son have lived in the refuge for one month.

6 - SINDY

Sindy was born in a major city in Pakistan. She is 25 years old and has achieved a BSc degree in Pakistan. Sindy was married in Pakistan and although her family and her husband's family knew each other, they were not related. It was however, an arranged marriage and a strong factor in the choice was that both had a degree education. Her husband had studied in England, where he was born and raised. Both Sindy and her husband are Muslim. Sindy came to England in 1999 and lived in a house with her husband and his parents. A year later she fell pregnant and had a daughter in May 2001. She never worked outside the home. She was married for one year and ten months. Sindy and her daughter have been living at the refuge for ten months.

7 – TINA

Tina was born in a rural district of Punjab, India. She is 26 years old and had an arranged marriage in India. She saw her husband briefly before the marriage. Five days after the marriage he returned to England. Tina joined him in England eight months later in 1998. Soon after her arrival in England her daughter was born. After a few weeks of giving birth Tina was forced to work outside the home by her husband. She had a cleaning job, working morning and evening shifts. Her husband was born and raised in England, he had been married previously and had four children. He did not have contact with his first wife and children. Tina lived with her husband and his mother in a run-down property with poor amenities. Both Tina and her husband are Sikh. She was married for four years. Tina and her daughter have lived in the refuge for five months, when she was asked to leave following a breach in the confidentiality regulations of the refuge. She now lives in a homeless hostel nearby.

Results

This was a small scale exploratory study on seven (South) Asian women and their children, that drew on their experiences of domestic violence. The findings indicate that there were particular cultural difficulties faced by these women.

All the women suffered social isolation and one of the greatest contributory factors to this was **lack of speaking the English language**. Because of this they were reluctant to call for assistance, therefore, their chances of obtaining help from an outside agency were low. In some circumstances, when the police were called, they chose to talk to the abuser or their relatives, who minimized the problem and put pressure on the women not to seek help.

None of the women interviewed had any **knowledge about their rights and restrictions** with regard to their personal freedom outside the family home, which made it difficult to seek assistance from agencies. Many were ignorant of their entitlements and some were deliberately kept that way. The belief that it was the husband's responsibility to take care of family issues resulted in the women being excluded from knowing their immigrant status and benefits. Majority of the women did not work and so were financially dependent on their husbands and in-laws to support them and their children. The few that did work, had no rights to their earnings and were compelled to transfer funds to their husbands and in-laws.

It seemed that the **'One Year Rule'** (then becoming the **Two Year Rule**) makes it extremely difficult for women who were formerly resident in India and Pakistan to leave violent marriages for fear of deportation. This leaves them with the stark choice of putting up with the abuse or returning to their countries of origin where there is a risk of bringing great dishonor to the woman's family. Two of the women interviewed underwent such threats, thereby allowing the spouse to maintain greater degree of control and power over his wife.

All the women expressed their reasons for remaining in the marriage was **for the sake of their children.** The husbands often threatened to prevent the children from leaving with their wives on the pretext that they "were British" like their fathers, and therefore had the right to remain in Britain and the wives were not, compelling the women to remain regardless.

The research was concerned with the nature of domestic violence and not with its extent. It is not possible to generalize from a sample of this size. However, it highlights some of the particular difficulties faced by (South) Asian women and their children in Britain.

CHAPTER 3
WHAT IS DOMESTIC VIOLENCE ?

Used in its widest sense, **'domestic violence'** encompasses child abuse, physical, psychological and sexual abuse, abuse between siblings, abuse between other family members and abuse and neglect towards the elderly and recently (2012) to include stalking. There appears to be no part of the world where domestic violence is unknown (United Nations Resource Manuel, June 1993).

Black feminists in the West have demanded that race, culture and religion be included into the analysis of violence against women. According to Mama (1989), this approach has challenged the views of Western feminists ;

' *who have focused narrowly on patriarchy and sexual oppression and therefore failed to consider class, racial and cultural oppressions.'*
Mama, A., p4 1989)

In Britain the term **'domestic violence'** is used to describe a number of actions and omissions (that can involve drugs and alcohol) that take place within the home or within relationships. For the purpose of this study I follow the description of **'domestic violence'** to mean: men's abuse of women in intimate relationships (Mullender and Morley, 1994).

Firstly, the word **'domestic'** has been criticized for its low prioritizing connection with the police - "it's just a domestic". There has been a national shift towards policing policy towards greater use of existing powers of arrest and the establishment of domestic violence units. Secondly, its false imagery of 'cosy domesticity' could trivialize the serious nature of the phenomena. Thirdly, 'domestic' implies that the violence occurs within a specific context – i.e., the home. However, the abuse could continue after the woman and child have left (Hester and Radford, 1996).

'Violence' as a word used in this manner is found to be ambiguous too and can include a range of behaviour which are in themselves not essentially considered 'violent'. For example, abuse can be – intimidation, threats, domination, economic domination (keeping a woman without money), isolation, deprivation of food, keeping women locked indoors, using her children to gain her compliance, emotional and sexual abuse. Additionally, abuse can also be reinforced or instigated by other family members, in-laws for example and contact with friends and family could be restrained or controlled. Also, the abuser may offer gifts to compensate the abuse shown followed by assurances that it would not occur again (Barron et al. 1992).

Occurrence of Domestic Violence

Domestic violence that may start off as minor attacks could escalate in intensity and frequency and may even result in death. Every year about 2.1 million people suffer domestic abuse – 1.4 million women (8.5% of the population). Every year more than 100,000 people in the U.K. are at risk of being murdered or seriously injured as a result of domestic violence. Women are more likely than men to be victims of severe domestic violence, with seven women a month killed by current or former partners in England and Wales. It is estimated that 130,000 children live in homes where there is a high risk of domestic violence with 62% of children directly harmed by perpetrators in addition to harm caused by witnessing abuse to others (Women's Aid 2015 survey).

Although these statistics show that domestic violence does exist, they are underrepresenting the problem. Some women are reluctant to report that they have been abused and may fail to report it because they feel ashamed or may be afraid or they may have a sense of family loyalty. Others may be terrified of disclosing the violence and involving outsiders and the state in what is considered to be a private and personal conflict. This could stem from lack of knowledge of availability of support services and fear of reprisals against the woman, i.e. children taken into care or for some women it may be the lack of language and therefore inability to communicate their needs.

The Refuge Movement

The refuge movement in England was started in the early 1970's providing protection for women and children suffering from domestic violence. Approximately 45,000 women and children were accommodated by refuge groups in England in 1992-3, of whom 28,000 were children (Women's Aid Federation of England, WAFE). Since its inception in the 1970's many refuges had few facilities for children. By 1986 the WAFE had introduced an aim to provide specific provision for children and by the 1990's most refuges saw the provision of services for children as a priority.

Although the majority of this study takes place with the refuge as a backdrop, it will not embark on issues or the politics of refuges in general. However, in order to illustrate the women and children's lives in the refuge, there is a chapter on a specialist (South) Asian Women's refuge provision and the women and children's experiences of it.

CHAPTER 4
MARRIAGE

(South) Asian Arranged Marriages

Arranged marriages has been practiced all over the world at some point. It is when parents or guardians determine who their child will marry. Whereas **forced marriage** is when an entry into marriage is accompanied by physical, mental and/or emotional duress and coercion from family members. Some literature indicates the differences between arranged and forced marriages can be fuzzy and inchoate (Caroll 1998). For the purpose of this study the focus will be on arranged marriage in South Asia, specifically in India and Pakistan. However, due to some recent cases of forced marriage in Britain, it is worth mentioning briefly some of the issues.

In a **forced marriage** one of the parties disagrees to the match but it goes ahead anyway, enforced by family elders. A woman in India or Pakistan could be forced to marry a (South) Asian or British Asian man from England because her family may agree it is a successful match. The Forced Marriage Unit indicates that forced marriage is prevalent in all (South) Asian communities although there is some evidence that it also occurs in some other communities (FCO & Home Office, 2005).

In 2012 a 16 year old British Asian girl went to Bedfordshire police for help. She told police that her family had threatened to send her abroad to marry, if she refused she would be taken " to Pakistan and shot and everybody back home would be told it was suicide". As a result she was made the subject of a Forced marriage Protection Order (the Government introduced the Forced Marriage (Civil Protection) Act 2007 which came into force in 2008). Despite this, she was forced to marry a man she had only met once and her mother and aunt were subsequently arrested for breaching the F.M.P.O. (The Telegraph, May 2013)

Other issues in 'arranged marriages'

Choudry (1996) describes how some women may find themselves in a position where they may have no knowledge or be misled about the husband-to-be's circumstances in England. In this instance she is particularly vulnerable if the marriage goes wrong. She cites the case of the woman who was married in Pakistan and found, on her arrival to England that her new husband had a wife and child and had expected them to all live together.

Sunita's husband was previously married to a British Asian girl and they had two children. When that marriage failed he left her and went to India to choose another wife from a Marriage bureau, marrying Sunita, but failed to severe ties with his first wife:

Sunita: 'I knew he was married before and had children, but when he married me he said he had no contact with them....but they were over most week-ends, even the weekdays they'd be over, often allowing his first wife to sleep over. Once they were in my bedroom, they were talking, I went and knocked on the door and went in and he told me to go out. In front of me he would hug and kiss the other ladies....' (his first wife and his girlfriend).

At this time economic underdevelopment in the East forced women to seek marriages arrangements abroad. Giving rise to commercial marriage bureaus. These arrangements with European/British Asian men promised expectations of a better economic life with possibilities for sending money home to poor relatives. This places women in vulnerable situations where they are seen as 'imported wives' with a minimum of civil rights and opportunities for abuse (Mama 1989).

An **arranged marriage** is seen as a contract between families rather than between two individuals (Ballard & Ballard 1977, Gillespie 1995), and both parties give their consent (Uddin & Ahmed 2000). It is the core of the prestige-gathering rituals of the Sikh life-cycle; with Pakistani Muslims preference is given by parents to cousin marriages. Shaw's study (2000) of Pakistani Muslims in Oxford, England found that the reasons given for marrying kin were for a daughter, to stay close to the family, minimizing the daughter's separation from the parents. It also serves to be forewarned about the groom's standard of living, personality and the mother-in-law's personality (often more important than a husband's).

Donnan's analysis (1985) of marriage preferences among the Dhund Abbasi of northeast Pakistan, states, that marriage with kin involves much more that cultural preferences. It is about the family's socio-economic status and reputation and the dynamics within the family. This suggests that marriage choices and the issues surrounding it must be understood within this framework of interconnectedness rather than the simplistic 'cultural preference'.

The idea of social advancement is another consideration for kin marriages. This is linked to marriages with relatives from Pakistan. For the British Asian it might be important to maintain contacts with kin in Pakistan, especially if they have business and property interests there. This ensures dependability and support. For the Pakistani kin, the advantages here mean that there will be the expectations of sending another family member to Britain, raising the prospect of socio-economic advantage (Shaw 2000).

Nina describe how her family married her to her uncle's son (cousin) in England:

Nina: 'My parents were poor, they married me off, I did not want to go back (to Pakistan) *to be a burden to them and bring disrepute on my family'*
Even after she did return to Pakistan following the abuse she said:
'After four months everyone in Pakistan were saying I'd better go back as it did not look good...'

Not only does close kin marriage provide opportunities to strengthen social relations and family ties but is seen as raising the status of a group of kin in relation to wider kin and neighbours in Pakistan. This encompasses not only in terms of monetary gains, i.e. property, business, land, but respectability and reputation as someone who honours his obligations.

Marrriage to kin are rare among the Punjabi Sikhs. However, sending a son or daughter to England for marriage raises the status of respectability and standing in the community. Migration abroad seems to have broadened the range of choice for many of the families in India, from a socio-economic advantage to the importance of family honour and obligations. On the other hand, from the British Asian view, it maintains a continuing commitment to the retention of roots in India and Pakistan and the advantage of a marriage to a traditional girl or boy not influenced by a Western environment who will uphold family honour and respect.

Sindy's experiences of 'fitting into the mould' of her husband's expectations of her, were frustrating and bewildering:

Sindy: 'He was telling me that he wanted a typical Asian culture woman...he was looking for a Pakistani girl who would know the culture, it was what his parents wanted as well. Otherwise, he would have married somebody from here...(England)'

I asked Tina about her arranged marriage:

Tina: '..My husband-to-be came with his sister and brother to meet me in India. They said they liked me but my family said it was up to me because he was 20 years older than me. But I agreed to marry him.

L.L.R.: *'Was there a dowry?* (the money, goods and estate that a woman brings to her husband in marriage)

Tina: 'Yes, after the wedding he asked me "well...what has your mother given you? Nothing, not even a bed sheet or a bed". My mother had to get money together to buy a bed, wardrobe and other things, just to show everybody that I was bringing things over not coming with nothing'.

None of the women in the study had love marriages. According to James (1974), an arranged marriage is often the ultimate test of the child's willingness to 'belong', with the respect and affection for the parents often outweighing the desire for freedom of choice and self-determination. Acceptance of arranged marriages also tend to deter parental criticism and family and community ostracism. Many find it strengthens traditional values, maintains family solidarity and establishes socio-economic advantages.

Many British Asians now are opting for 'semi-arranged' marriages, which means they would have more of a say in the choice of partner. Ballard and Ballard (1977) found that established relationships that develop (between a girl and boy) may be presented as if it were a conventionally arranged agreement, with many young (South) Asians wishing to have greater opportunities in decisions surrounding their marriages (Taylor 1976, Gillespie 1995).

Nevertheless, it seems that the evidence to date suggests that arranged marriages remain important and are likely to continue, especially among the cousin marriages of the Pakistani community, when both socio-economic security and family honour play a part. It may be likely that British born Sikhs will have more say in their marriage choices, but as long as the commitment remains between relatives in India/Pakistan and Britain, marriage arrangement will continue.

CHAPTER 5
THE VIOLENCE

Six women out of the seven interviewed had sustained physical and mental abuse. The seventh woman was in the refuge with her son because he had been exposed to phonographic material and due to the child's inappropriate behaviour, there were allegations of sexual abuse. One of the six women was almost exclusively abused physically and mentally by her in-laws. In fact the men in that household did not readily get involved with any of the physical abuse on a regular basis, choosing less obvious behaviour to undermine, humiliate and isolate the woman instead.

In this study I have categorized the women's accounts of the violence under the various actions and behaviour exhibited by their abusers. However, domestic violence does not limit itself to a particular class, ethnic culture or social group but is instigated by men against women across the social spectrum (Smith 1989, Hague & Malos 1993). What differs is the individual experience of domestic violence as a result of these different contexts.

The Beginning

Some of the women in the study reported physical and mental abuse at the start of their marriages. The first violent incident usually occurs after the relationship has become serious and committed, often after marriage (Hester & Radford 1992). At this point the woman is now perceived to 'belong' to the man.

Seema had just arrived from India to join her husband and their baby. On their first day together:

Seema: '...we went to his house where he lived....there was no food in the house or anything. I said that we needed to get some food and things for the baby. Immediately he slapped me around a few times and then said —"who do you think you are? Coming over here...you should go and buy your own food and shopping, don't ask me to get things for you." He said he did not want any responsibilities and did not want to do anything.'

The abuse experienced was not always metered out by the husband, often the in-laws encouraged (the husband) and even instigated the abuse. Nina describes her first week in her new home:

Nina: 'I was soon told – "You are in the house and these are your duties, like cleaning, cooking and you will keep quiet and you will not talk to anybody." In the house there were five sisters-in-law, one brother-in-law and parents-in-law.'

Choudry (1996) found that in many cultures, as in (South) Asian cultures it was imperative to develop a cordial relationship with the mother-in-law. It is the mother-in-law that rules the household and in her absence her role is taken on by any older sisters-in-law. Most of the violence and abuse that Nina endured was from the in-laws. In the beginning before she had any children she was warned by one sister-in-law:

*Nina: 'She said – "…there will be no name following your marriage…no child to carry the name of the family on, we are going to make sure of that." (*meaning that Nina would not be entitled to use her husband's name neither will any children born to her)

In the beginning, Nina's husband was fine with her but would not speak to her when his sisters were present.

Nina: 'He hardly spoke to me anyway, the only times he would speak would be when we were upstairs in the bedroom, even then it was so quiet that nobody would think there was anyone in the room.'

Soon after Sindy came to England to join her husband:

L.L.R.: 'Tell me what happened when you came to England.'

*Sindy: 'He just wanted to control me. He did not want me to go out, he did not allow me to speak to anyone, he did not allow me to pick up a phone, those sort of things. It's like he just wanted to pressure me and after three months he sent me back to Pakistan. He said I was not settling properly here (*England)…*I was confused, you know, come here, go there. He just wanted to confuse my life…he said I was to learn how to budget and how to run a house, how can I learn over there..(*Pakistan) *when I need to be here, I came back to England after three months.'*

Pregnancy

Many women find that the abuse is also likely to begin at the time of their pregnancy or when the children are young. Sometimes the violence may increase at this time raising their vulnerability (Hoff 1990, Phal 1985).

Nina tried to hide the fact that she was pregnant for fear of reprisals from the in-laws:

Nina: 'They did not know that I was pregnant. I did not tell anybody in the house…not even my husband, the mother-in-law and the others, nobody knew. Even when I was five months pregnant I used to wear baggy jumpers, nobody really noticed. If they found out they would hit me because the older sister-in-law already said that there would not be any name carrying in this house, so if they found out they might have tried to hurt me.'

They eventually discovered the pregnancy and did not deter from abusing Nina. For example, they prevented her from keeping her ante-natal appointments saying she was just making excuses to get out of the house, they felt there was nothing wrong with her. Even when Nina went into labour, they relentlessly continued:

Nina: 'I was in a lot of pain, they kept saying it was an excuse, they made me mop the floor, as you know it is a big house. When I finished I just threw everything down and cried. The mother-in-law ignored me saying "you are just like that!" and went to have her bath. I began screaming, nobody came.'

Nina managed to alert her husband who got her to hospital on time to deliver her first child. Throughout her pregnancies, Nina was not allowed to rest, even when she was getting contractions. She would sit for a minute till it passed and then carry on with the housework – *"nobody cared"* she reports.

When Sindy fell pregnant her husband emphasized that he did not want the baby and tried to convince her to have an abortion. When that did not work he became physically violent with her. He did not want the responsibility of caring for a wife and child. He also spent longer hours at work. Sindy says:

Sindy: 'He just kept beating me, even in the last month (of pregnancy) *when I was nine months he beat me and when the baby was born he became worse. I had to have stitches…he's a psycho, basically.'*

Sunita explains that her abusive experiences began when she was pregnant :

Sunita: 'When I fell pregnant, my mother-in-law said to me, "…he had a girlfriend for three years." My husband did not want the baby and wanted me to have an abortion…he said "have an abortion or I will divorce you." He said that in front of the doctor. I was always frightened he would do something. When I would not have an abortion he kept saying "have it now and we will try for a baby in two years." I said "you've already got two children and I only want the one." I did not agree to an abortion so, every few days he would start an argument and hit me.'

When Sunita's husband's children from his first marriage visited, they would stay the night, sleeping in Sunita's bedroom, she would have to sleep on the sofa even though she was pregnant, she was not given a choice.

Abuse of Children

Some of the earliest research on domestic violence and child abuse was studied in the United States. From this it was discovered that in the context of domestic violence, child abuse was most likely to take place, making domestic violence a strong indicator of child abuse (Hester, Pearson & Harwin 2000).

When Nina arrived home with her new baby she was not allowed to breast feed the baby, because she had work to do in the house and could not spend work time breast feeding. She was allowed to make up the bottle feeds for the in-laws to feed. In fact she was not allowed to bottle feed the baby. When the second child came along she was taken out of her husband's room and told by the mother-in-law to use the room downstairs with the new baby. The older child was now taken upstairs to share a room with his father and grandfather. By moving to the downstairs room with the new baby Nina was able to give the baby the night feeds (no other family member wanted their sleep disrupted) and sometimes if there was no one around she would do a daytime feed. Generally, most of the feeds were done by the rest of the family.

Nina describes the feeding routine:

'...if they went out they'd take the older child with them but the baby would be kept in a locked room until it was time to feed. I would stand outside and say "he's crying...."'

L.L.R.: 'Who had the key to the room?'

Nina: 'It was always the mother-in-law, or whoever else was in charge...to open the door at feed time. The baby was kept under lock and key till he was about a year old, that's only because he would be a bit mobile then...'

L.L.R.; 'So, no stimulation for the baby? Did they play and talk to the baby?'

Nina: 'No, the children were not allowed to have anything, no toys, no books, only when they got older, they watched T.V.'

Neelam was at the refuge because her three year old son was found to be displaying inappropriate behaviour at the playgroup. It was discovered that Neelam's husband was watching pornographic videos and allowing the child to participate. The small boy was consequently displaying 'acting out', behaviour he had observed in the videos. Initially, Neelam said that she was not aware that this was going on and it was only when her son's playgroup staff informed her that she became alerted and when her husband visited his mother she searched the house and came across the videos and magazines.

Neelam: '*I was never aware of when he* (husband) *watched them, but if my son was upset like this* (the son would sometimes become very noisy/agitated) *he would give him a magazine to look at and that would keep him quiet, or if the video* (ponographic) *was on he did not care if the child was in the room, he would just let him watch it.*'

It is uncertain whether Neelam's husband forced the child to watch the films, Neelam denies this, but there were questions asked about inappropriate behaviour between the husband and child. In this case the abuse was directed at the child. Neelam added that the playgroup staff remarked to her about her son's behaviour:

Neelam: '*The staff at the playgroup noticed that if any dolls were present my son would strip the doll's clothing off, and they said his behaviour with the doll was inappropriate.*'

Neelam's child had been going to the playgroup for 7 – 8 months when the staff started noting her son's behaviour, hence, they informed Social Services who then had a meeting and decided that the child would be taken away from her if she did not leave the house with him. She was advised to go to a refuge.

Seema's husband has frequently hit her and soon he started on the child, who was three years old at the time. On one occasion he bruised her daughter badly on the legs and arms. The health visitor reported it to social services and subsequently, the husband admitted the injuries were non-accidental. Seema describes how her husband restricted her daughter's activities:

Seema: '*...my daughter is quite sensitive anyway, because she was never allowed to play or do what other children do. When he was at home she was told to sit there* (keep still). *She was never allowed to look out of the windows, if she was caught looking out of the windows, he would then start putting wallpaper or paper on the windows, so she would not be able to look out. There was only the kitchen window which did not have paper on it and she used to sit there and look out...you know, watch the other children play or whatever. Then she was caught looking out and she was in trouble...*(Seema cries, tape stopped).

L.L.R.; '*Did she not play in the playground with other children?*
Seema: '*No, she was not allowed out.*'

Seema's daughter was ill during this interview, with the 'flu. When the other children in the refuge knocked on the door to ask her to play with them, she immediately jumped out of bed and went with them. It seemed that although she was unwell she did not want to miss out on the fun and games anymore. Her mother confirmed this.

Nina's daughter was subjected to abuse from the in-laws because of her gender and birthdate, she was born on the 25th December.

Nina: 'As she was born on Christmas day they (the in-laws) *were saying that it's not right her born on this day – bad luck, bad luck. They did not like her at all. They used to hit her and used to wish that she was dead,* (because she was female) *and she got marks all over her body where they have abused her.'*

L.L.R.: 'When did they start hitting her ?'

Nina: 'When I came back from hospital'

L.L.R.: 'As a baby?'

Nina: ' Yes, they used to hit her on her back, the tiny baby coming home on her first day from hospital. They used to get hold of her hands and put them in her mouth...you know.. in her mouth, they would say she would die. They were giving her cold milk..'

However, Nina's father-in-law was fond of her daughter, he would often spend time talking to her. She was about two years old at this time. The other women in the family were jealous of this relationship and threatened to harm the little girl if she told tales about them. On one occasion after the father-in-law had gone up to bed they took Nina's little daughter to a room at the back of the house and physically abused her. Nina describes the incident:

Nina: 'There were three doors, the living room door, the kitchen door and a bathroom door. They took her right to the end, into the bathroom and then hit her. She was hurt badly, bruised, her eyes were blackened. As soon as they finished with her they told me to clean her up, she was covered with blood. Then the teachers at the nursery wanted to know where she got the marks on her body. The next day one of the sisters-in-law went to the nursery and said she had a party at home and fell and hurt herself. Nobody in the family wanted to take her back to the nursery, so then she was abused even more, because she was at home. All her neck was scratched, as if she'd been shredded.'

Kelly and Radford (1988, 1996) suggests that it is important to take the experiences of survivors of domestic violence as a starting point, to provide a better understanding of the issues and enable a development of a definition that includes the behaviour described by the survivors. Kelly call this a 'continuum of violence.'

Deprivation of food

Only one woman in the study spoke about her experiences of hunger and food deprivation. The others did not mention it as being a problem. As the women were the preparers of the family meals, most had the opportunity to eat as and when needed. Apart from periods of emotional and physical upheavals, when their appetites would have been at a minimum.

Nina outlines the mealtime rituals in her house:

Nina: '*At mealtimes I was making all the chapattis* (a thin unleavened round bread, usually Indian food)

And preparing all the ingredients for the curry, but I was not allowed to cook it. The mother-in-law or one of the sisters-in-law cooked it. It was only like the first week when I arrived from Pakistan that I was able (allowed) *to have a meal with the family or even on my own. Because there was always housework to do, there was always washing and cleaning.*'

L.L.R.: '*When did you eat?*'

Nina: '*…I made chapatti for myself and by the time I got around to eating it was cold, I was tired and when I was going to eat…sometimes I would eat when nobody was around, I would quickly have something to eat, because if I was ever caught eating or drinking they would start calling me names and all sorts… "eating like a dog, drinking like a dog – do your work" they'd say "this is not your father's house…" I would say… "okay, it's not my father's house but I'm working here, why should I go to my father's house to eat?" Then, I would get a beating, they would gang up on me and hit me.*'

On many occasions Nina reports, that the in-laws extended this food deprivation behaviour towards her daughter:

Nina: '*I was sitting on the floor and feeding the baby girl, the mother-in-law came and kicked the plate and said "what do you think this is, your house? Coming here and giving the child food to eat." And then they just got hold of me, they used any excuse to hold me down and kick and punch me.*'

I asked Nina if her sons were preferentially treated at mealtimes.

Nina: '*…as they were getting older, they were able to sit with their father and grandfather and eat..*'

L.L.R.: '*The men were always eating together?*'

Nina: '*Yes, the father the grandfather and the two male children…they would get everything to eat…but only when the father and grandfather were around, as soon as the men were out, the women would pick on the boys. If the boys said that aunty or granny was hitting me, as soon as the men leave, the boys would get it.*'

*With the girl, she would be sat in the corner by the grandmother (*Nina demonstrates how the mother-in-law pinned the child in the corner so she was unable to move)

…they would all be eating and they might give a little bit to her or she was just told to sit

quietly...'

Nina reported that the family never sat at a table to eat. There were sofas and armchairs placed against the walls of the room with the table in the corner. The family members served themselves from dishes placed on the table and sat in the surrounding seating. The children in the house were never given plates to eat from, instead they ate their food placed in newspapers. The adults had their chapattis (Indian bread) in a *chingay* (wicker bowl) and the liquid foods (curries) in a plate.

Hellman (2001) states that food is more than just a source of nutrition, playing a number of roles, embedded in social, religious and economic aspects of life. He describes it as having symbolic meaning and expression, making food an important aspect of how a society organizes itself. Food consumed in the presence of other people (communal meal) can be very informative about the participants; their relationship with one another and with their society. Because these mealtimes involve a ritual aspect, it is hence controlled by the norms of a particular society, i.e., the preparation, cooking, clearing up, the seating arrangement in relation to others, the timing etc. Hellman views this as a complicated *language*, when interpreted, can reveal a great deal about the relationships and values of the participants, gender roles, familial hierarchy and many other social roles. There are numerous symbolic rituals, practices and beliefs and taboos attached to food and their preparation, too numerous to mention here.

However, Nina's experiences are not the norms of (South) Asian meal rituals. The withholding of nutrition seems to indicate that she is perceived as non-existent, not a family member. She is allowed to prepare the ingredients, but not permitted to cook the meal. Meaning that there is a status aspect to the cooking. Nina has no status, she is not allowed to partake of the meal in the family's presence or be seen to be eating or drinking. The abusive *language* spoken here can only mean that these oppressive conditions are intended to weaken her resistance, through malnutrition, making it easier to brutalize her into further subordination. The interpretation of *'deprivation'* here means an inability to obtain available food due to unequal distribution of resources.

Abuse by other family members

For many (South) Asian women, after marriage they move into the husband's parents' home (this could also apply to many other cultures). Usually the husband's father or elder brother head the household, making formal decisions in the family. Amongst the women there is a hierarchy of age and status, the older women have authority over the younger women (Shaw 2000). The mother-in-law is the female head of the house, with the husband's older sisters and brothers having higher status than the new bride. Only the husband's youngest brother will share an equal status with the new bride.

Many of the women that were interviewed felt that the violence that they endured was instigated, exacerbated, encouraged or ignored by the in-laws and in fact the in-laws were sometimes the perpetrators of the violence themselves, thereby multiplying the violence endured by these women.

In Preeya's case, her father-in-law and mother-in-law used to physically abuse her quite regularly, sometimes her brother-in-law joined in:

Preeya: 'I told my brother-in-law I was phoning India and he said "Why?" and there was a little argument there, he said something to me and I answered back and he hit me…that was the first time my brother-in-law hit me. But my mother-in-law and father-in-law used to regularly hit me and swear at me.'

On the day she left the house following such a beating she was in great pain, but had to drag herself to work for fear of more abuse if she remained home. As traditional (South) Asian wives, these women were expected to live in the family home and cook, clean and serve their in-laws and husband. Preeya worked hard at her job outside the home and was left to do all the household chores too:

Preeya: 'I worked in a factory from 5a.m. to 7p.m. seven days a week. If at home, I was cleaning, any mark anywhere and I was in trouble, so that is why I was always at work. But then it changed and I had to work six days a week, one day off. Every week-end they'd be visitors at home. I'd be in the kitchen cooking, cleaning, housework and not get to bed until 1 or 2 a.m., and then up at 5a.m. again and go to work.'

For some of the women, as in Sindy's case, when her husband was violent she got no support from her mother-in-law due to the fact that she too was abused by her husband. Thereby upholding conformist elements in the name of respectability.

Sindy: 'They, (the husband's family) were on his side all the time. The mother-in-law said "..he's your husband, if he's beating you or doing anything you have to accept these things. We all had to put up with such things. My husband did beat me.".'

Restricted contacts & social isolation

Many of the women in the study raised the issue of restricted contacts with the outside world. Choudhry (1996) described how a woman in her study was locked up in her house everyday by her husband and was not even allowed to look out of the window in case she was seen.

Nina was never allowed to go out unless accompanied by one of the in-laws and that was only to the doctor's surgery and when she had her babies in hospital.

Nina: 'When the family went out I was left with one of the sisters–in-law, who had a disability. The sister-in-law was told by the family – "you stay at home and look after her (Nina)*and watch what she is doing".'*

Nina had no idea where she lived, she did not know the name of the road, in fact she had never seen the end of her road. On one occasion she escaped:

Nina: 'Once they beat me so much that I just went out and kept walking and walking. I did not know where I was going, I just cried and carried on walking. The next thing I knew I was just bundled into a car by the sister-in-law, they had followed me and dragged me back. I got more beatings for running away, this time from my husband.'

I asked Nina as she had lived here (U.K.) for eleven years, how did she not know her address or her phone number?

Nina: '…when any post came to the house, there was not even a letter I was allowed to look at. They had this big box and all the mail that came would be kept in the box. Any letters they did not want would be shredded.'

L.L.R.: 'What about your family's letters?'

Nina: 'Letters from my family were always torn, I was never able to see them. They used to read it…I was never allowed to use the phone or write to my family back in Pakistan.'

Preeya's contact with her own family in India were equally controlled and monitored:

Preeya: 'I was not encouraged to use the phone to call my parents at all. If I ever did, they would be sitting and listening in to what I was saying. In the five years I had been over here I never told my parents that he (husband) *was hardly ever at home or these are the problems I've had..'*

Often contacts with any friends or relatives were prohibited as Seema found out :

Seema: '…he used to leave home for work very early in the morning and get home about 8p.m. All day I would be on my own. I used to visit an aunt who lived close by, but when he found out I was in trouble again. He did not want me to see them and they were not allowed to come over. He used to phone in the daytime to make sure I was in and drop in at home to make sure nobody else was visiting.'

One of the contributing factors to the social isolation that many of these women face in the U.K. is language. Following domestic violence, the woman would be unable to make a phone call for assistance because of her inability to speak English, diminishing her chances of obtaining outside help. Choudhry (1996) cites how one woman called for help and had to communicate through her 10 year old daughter.

In many of the cases in this study, it was the neighbours who called the police for assistance. Generally, neighbours abhor getting involved for fear of reprisals from the husband or for interfering in what is still often considered a *'private'* affair.

Sometimes movements within the household were restricted, as Sunita found out:

Sunita: 'At home I was not allowed to go out, I was not allowed to use the phone, I was not allowed any money....I was not allowed to watch television, I was not allowed in this room, I can only stay in that room...'

Sunita's restrictions extended to the bedroom, too. When the husband went to work, the bedroom was locked and she was not allowed to go back in, even to lie down (she was pregnant at this time). She was told to lie on the sofa in the lounge. However, she was never allowed to spend much time resting. The bedroom was unlocked on her husband's return in the evening. Even visits to the doctor were carefully monitored :

Sunita: 'When I went to the doctor for a check-up, the mother-in-law was always with me or the husband, so I could never complain about anything that was happening in the house.'

A significant amount of women interviewed were ignorant of their rights and entitlements. There was little or no opportunity for them to explore this avenue and besides, it was in the husband's and his family's interest to keep them dependent and therefore under control. Many did not have relatives or friends that they could turn to in England and the ones that did stated that they did not wish to burden them with their problems.

Economic Domination

Three out of the seven women interviewed worked outside the home. Preeya worked in a factory for long hours 6 – 7 days a week:

Preeya: 'When I started working I had my own bank account and the money/salary went into that. I was working long hours and I got good money. When my husband noticed that I got good money and the money was building up he wanted a joint account. I said I did not, the money is here and that I was not going to run off with it, but they (the in-laws and husband) forced me to sign up for a joint account. Then when I left the home, they tried to get the money but I went to the bank and told them to freeze my account. They have been trying to get hold of it…that case is still going on.'

Seema describes her experience:

Seema: 'I would get up at 4.30 a.m. to go to work. He (husband) *would not take any money off me, I had good wages. Instead he said "why don't we save up and get a mortgage?". He went with me and opened a bank account in my name only. He said we need two names for a mortgage. The rent, food, bills, bus fares was direct debited to my account only. After any shopping he would look at each receipt to see what I had bought. There would be a couple of hundred pounds left over,* (after paying the bills every month) *so I would buy little bits of furniture, because when I first married him there was no furniture, not even a bed. He spent all his money on alcohol..'*

Tina's husband too spent his money on drink, he was an alcoholic who spent his disability benefit on drink. Tina worked as a cleaner, a couple of hours in the morning and evening. The house needed extensive maintenance and repairs. A few weeks after Tina's arrival she gave birth to her daughter, six weeks later her husband sent her back to work. She would walk to work and back. Gradually, with the money she earned she was able to buy some household necessities; a bed, fridge and carpeting. Her husband soon put a stop to this and demanded her money be given to him, he wanted to buy land in India. Apparently, he also obtained money in this manner from his first wife. Once the house was built in India (that both wives had substantially contributed to and that neither had a stake in), he sent his mother back to India to live in it and he resumed claiming his mother's benefits in the U.K., illegally.

The evidence of some of the women in this study contradicts the Western feminist analysis of domestic violence which links it to women's *'economic marginalization and concomitant dependence'* on their husband's income (Mama 1989). There were some women who were abused by the men who depended on them, indicating that men would continue this abusive domination despite their dependence on the woman. In fact this *'independence'* that these women enjoyed was probably an exacerbating factor for some of the men and a source of antagonism. This suggests that the behaviour displayed by the men who seem unable to live up to the patriarchal image towards the women they are dependent on, could be likened to a kind of socio-economic jealousy that parallel's sexual jealousy.

The Other Relationships

A significant amount of the women named the affairs that their husbands were having as another factor in the disintegration of their marriages. Seema's aunt who had arranged her marriage had three sons. One of them had separated from his wife. The wife was having an affair with Seema's husband.

Seema: 'My husband was spending all day, every day with her. He was not going to work like he said he was, he was spending every day with her, drinking and getting drunk and then coming home. He was then trying to send me back to India. He said he did not want me, not the responsibility. He was married before and had a lot of girlfriends and he is not the kind to settle down.'

Nina's husband had a call girl arrangement with his other taxi driver friends:

Nina: 'This girl used to come to the house, (South) Asian girl, born here, (U.K.) and my sister-in-law used to say she was their friend, they spoke in English. I knew there were girls at the corner of the road he would pick up and take them out...like prostitutes. His friend had a house and so they would pick up these girls, ten of them and then get these men and eh...

L.L.R.: 'Party?'

Nina: 'Yes, a call girl arrangement. All these taxi drivers who had some minor problems at home or upsets, my husband would arrange all this...'

L.L.R.: 'A party with the call girls?'

Nina: 'Yes, they would choose and pay so much. There would be a gang of girls, mixed – Asian and English, my husband would pick them up and take them. He said he was a taxi driver and so was able to pick them up.'

Sunita's mother-in-law informed her that her husband had a continuing relationship with a girl for three years. Her sister-in-law confirmed it, adding that although it was a stormy and violent relationship, he would spend many of his days with her instead of working. Sunita insists that her husband also spent a substantial amount of time with his first wife, who was a frequent visitor to the house, during the day and sometimes staying overnight.

Sindy was convinced that her husband's behaviour betrayed her:

Sindy: 'When I was pregnant he was out most of the time, hardly ever home. He had girlfriends and he would not come home at night....I know he's not bothered whether I come back to him or not, because he has other relationships.'

The Law

Making direct contact with the police is extremely difficult for (South) Asian women who suffer domestic violence. Firstly, they fear that involving the police reflects negatively on their honour and standing in the community. Secondly, they have a problem with language.   Many of the women interviewed spoke of the police involvement as ineffective, because the police when called, spoke to the abuser or his collaborators (husband and relatives) who would minimize the issues, put pressure on the woman not to seek help and encourage them to deny any issue at all – *"just nod your head and smile.."*, Seema's husband ordered her to do.

Seema: 'The police would come in but I would not be aware of what they were saying and what the husband was saying, but they would soon leave.   Because they all spoke English and I did not understand what was going on.'

Sometimes the women got help from neighbours and friends who called the police on their behalf. Following a violent episode from her in-laws, Preeya went to a friend's house instead of going to work:

Preeya: 'I stayed at my friend's house and from there she reported it to the police…about what had happened.'

In the meantime the in-laws had reported her missing saying that she had left home and taken their gold (jewellery).   The police investigated Preeya, but found no evidence of the missing gold jewellery.

Seema too had help from neighbours who coaxed her to inform the police of her husband's continual violence and that they would support her.   On one occasion she did call the police, she managed to alert them with her limited English.   They came to the house and had to break the door to get in.   Three policemen kept asking her if she was alright. She was instructed by her husband not to reply, but in the end they arrested him following his attack on the officers.

They could be problems and time delays for the police to gain access to a female Urdu or Punjabi speaking interpreter, allowing a period in which the woman can be persuaded not to pursue the complaint.

Seeking assistance from the Domestic Violence Unit can also deter some (South) Asian women, with the answering machine (especially out-of-hours) messages that they can neither understand nor can they leave a message of their own.   There are specific domestic violence helplines to cater for a variety of ethnic minority groups and leaflets or cards containing phone numbers can pose additional dangers for the women, if discovered by the abusers.

The Legislation

At the time of the study, the immigration legislation in force was the 'One Year Rule' (OYR). The OYR policy states that the spouses of persons entitled to stay in the U.K., (the husbands in this study) who do not themselves have such an entitlement (the wives in this study) are allowed to stay for an initial period of 12 months and only if they have the intention of living permanently with their spouse and are supported without recourse to public funds. In 1999 the government announced a concession to the OYR allowing women whose marriages have broken down as a result of domestic violence to stay in the U.K. if they could prove that domestic violence was the cause for the break down.

The standard of proof required to demonstrate domestic violence was very high and very few women were able to meet it. In November 2002 the Government extended the type of evidence required to prove domestic violence, however, the issue of No Recourse to Public Funds (NRPF) remained.

'The One Year Rule states, that if for any reason the marriage fails during the probationary one year (now two year) *period, the normal expectation is that the spouse will return to his or her country, as the purpose for which the spouse was admitted no longer exists. The marriage to obtain settlement to which they would otherwise not be entitled. Compassionate factors can be taken into account if marriages do fail and consideration can be given to applications to remain under some other part of the immigration rules'*
(Choudry 1996)

This leaves (South) Asian women experiencing violence in their marriage compelled to remain, despite the abuse, for fear of being deported and bringing shame and dishonour on their own families in their country. It could also be used by the husband to threaten and coerce his wife to remain for the sake of the children, as they would be prevented from taking the children with them and so maintaining the husband's power and control over the abused woman.

Seema and her daughter went back to India, after a particularly violent argument with her husband and on his insistence both mother and daughter left the family home:

Seema: 'After I'd been away for four weeks, he reported to the police that I had gone off with his daughter and he did not know where I had gone. The police went to my aunt's house to enquire if I had gone back to India. He then followed me to India and when he got there he said he wanted my daughter back…..in India he paid the police and said I had his daughter and he was from England and he now wants her back. You give the police money in India and they will do anything. They said that he was British, the daughter would go to him…solicitors in India said that, he's British, the daughter is British, he'll have the daughter. In India the law says that the child will stay with the father, whatever happens, the mother would not get them. So that is why I came back, to get my daughter.

CHAPTER 6
THE EFFECTS OF DOMESTIC VIOLENCE ON THE CHILDREN

The impact of domestic violence on children varies enormously. Some children are more effected than others and it is generally found that children who have lived in a context of domestic violence have more problems adjusting to life then children from non-violent homes (Hester, Pearson & Harwin 2000).

The experiences of domestic violence and the reaction of the child to them will be unique to each child, making it difficult to discern the impact by resulting behaviour as certain behaviour would also occur in children experiencing other forms of abuse and neglect (Holden & Ritchie 1991).

Most of the research available in this area derives from studies conducted in refuges and the child support services. However, according to Kelly (1994), much of the refuge samples are over representative of children from the lower socio-economic groups, as do the samples from the child support services. Additionally, many children living with domestic violence do not come to the attention of any of the services (Hallett 1995).

Because the source of most of the data in this study is obtained from the mothers of the children (also pointed out in Fantuzzo & Linquist's study 1998), I am aware that there are differences between the mother's and child's perceptions of the impact of living with domestic violence. It is important to understand children's experiences and as far as possible they should be allowed to express their feelings.

None of the mothers in the study discussed their children's feelings with them…They resolutely believed that now the children were out of harm's way, they would be happier and did not wish to remind them of the trauma.

When Preeya left the home she was unable to take her daughter with her. She was however, reunited with her three weeks later following a solicitor's intervention. I asked her how her daughter felt about her leaving the home:

Preeya: 'When I left the home, they (husband and in-laws) said to my daughter, "Your mum is dead and she is not coming back", that really upset my daughter…even now she says, "mum, they used to beat you", she knows why we left.

I asked Preeya how her daughter felt about staying in the refuge.

Preeya: 'She's not too bad, children don't always say anything but they play around with other children as well...she is quite happy in school, too...'
I persevered in questioning about her daughter's feelings.

Preeya: 'She is usually quite scared...she has been like that since we've come away from the home and even at school the teachers have said she is always scared, so I explained to the teachers. In the beginning she was very clingy and did not want me out of her sight. At night she was upset with bad dreams and all...she was always following me around.'

I asked if her daughter had opened up to her, talked about her feelings and had she noticed any changes in behaviour.

Preeya: 'When she comes back from visits (to the in-laws) *she says they say "your mummy is no good, your mummy is dirty...". So she comes back and tells me, but she'd turn around and say to them "no, no, my mummy is nice".*
Sometimes her behaviour is changed ...she gets a bit upset when the in-laws say things, but generally she is okay.'

Seema had spoken to me earlier (in my health visitor role) about the nightmares her daughter was experiencing. I asked her about it now.

Seema: 'My daughter is usually fine, but I think the reason for some of these dreams is maybe when somebody (in the refuge) *has mentioned about their husband or dad which to her, 'dad' is like a bad thing...a monster. When she hears it...she does not tell me, but those are the nights that she is up, scary nights where there are things on the window...'.*

Seema described how her daughter kept getting up during the night and running to the window and looking out, she says, almost to make sure she was at the refuge and not at home. There were issues about Seema's husband disciplining her daughter when she looked out of the windows in their house. These nightmares revolving around windows, appeared to be connected to those events.

Studies in the U.K. on the extent of the impact of domestic violence on children from the perspective of professionals, mothers and refuge workers have all reported similar findings to those described by the women in this study. Moore's (1975) study on matrimonial violence, found that the effects the children sustained were feelings of anxiety, difficulties in school and being silent and withdrawn. In Evason's (1982) study 72% of the women verified that some of the nightmares and nervous behaviour of their children were the result of living with domestic violence. Similarly, the mothers in Hester and Radford's (1996) research included having nightmares and delayed development among the effects that domestic violence had on their children.

Nina, whose daughter has suffered terrible and prolonged abuse from the in-laws, did not report any adverse repercussions from this, just stating that her daughter is just so happy to be at the refuge and that there is a change for the better. As long as Nina does not mention the sisters-in-law's names, as the mere mention of them frightens the child. I asked if she noticed any changes in behaviour since she has been at the refuge.

Nina: 'Every time she ate when she was there (at home) *she would be sick, and she'd be sick again if they started swearing at her…through fright. They used to drag her by her hair* (the in-laws). *Now she is fine.*

L.L.R.: ' Does she have any nightmares?'

Nina: ' Here she sleeps well, she sleeps all night; but when she was at home she would not sleep. If she got up…normally if children get up they'd wake up the whole house, but she would not. She would always pretend she was asleep, even though she would wake up, she would not get out of bed. She would hide under the blankets for fear they'd hit her.
She was still sleeping in a cot at four years old. She was so frightened, she was not eating properly. In her cot she chewed away all the paint, it was also because she was hungry and too frightened to ask for food'.

L.L.R.: 'Any of that behaviour now?'

Nina: 'Since she has left the house she has never once been sick. She has slept all night, no problems. She is quite happy and asks for all sorts of foods.'

Binney et al.'s (1981) study on refuge life described how the mothers in their study reported that since they came to the refuge their children were less jumpy, less withdrawn and not clingy and now played more easily with the other children. There were health improvements in previous nervous illnesses and asthma and habits like bed-wetting and nail-biting were on the decrease.

In this study, many of the women were over-protective of their children, indulging them with extra attention and time. Some felt guilty about putting their children through the trauma and compensated by disciplining them less than they normally would, with children sometimes 'playing up' and copying other children's negative behaviour, an issue also found in Binney et al.'s sample. They found that as the children became less withdrawn, they were more boisterous and noisy, the women complained that they found their children sometimes difficult to cope with because of the disruption of their usual patterns of discipline.

Reviewing the literature, there is clear evidence from a variety of studies that domestic violence can have a detrimental impact on children, but more research needs to be done on children of the ethnic minority population.

This chapter has shown some of the effects of domestic violence on the children in the study sample. Although it is acknowledged that the information obtained was from the mother's perspective of the child's view and feelings, it would be important to explore the children's view directly and to be able to discuss the issues of domestic violence with the child. This may seem too directive, but if handled sensitively it could dispel the taboo that children have, that is, that adults want to keep 'domestic violence' issues 'a secret', overcoming this it could be the first step in the healing process of the child.

CHAPTER 7
THE REFUGE

This chapter will focus on –
a) the refuge provision (as there is a great deal of differentiation between types of refuges and how they meet the needs of the women and children)
b) Some of the women's comments on their refuge experiences.

It will aim to gather enough information to gain a fuller picture of the next stage of the women and children's life following the domestic violence they experienced. It will not involve their experiences with other statutory agencies. However, it is interesting to note that other studies that examined black women's involvement with the statutory sector (Mama 1989) have indicated that due to increase corporatization of the British state, public services can become coercive rather than supportive. This often leads to a service delivery that appears to be overly concerned over eligibility and exclusion when dealing with black women.

While I don't deny that relevant agencies ought to respond more effectively to the needs of black women and to identify gaps in their service delivery sensitive to this group, as clearly the evidence has indicated this, the experiences recounted in this study have identified a resounding number of positive elements. Hence, I would like to think that due to some of these earlier studies, statutory and non-statutory bodies have acted on some of the recommendations.

The Refuge Experience

The refuge in the study opened in 1995 and was specifically for (South) Asian women and children. It was fully staffed by South and British Asian women. The refuge accepted referrals from The Samaritans, The Domestic Violence Unit, Social Services, the homeless sector and outside agencies and organizations, i.e. various other refuges, nationwide. Referrals could also be made by the refuge to other refuges if the woman requests it, for example, if there is a preferred area or there is an issue of unsuitability of a refuge or if there is a lack of accommodation in the current refuge.

What the refuge requires from the women and children

The women are required to fit the following criteria to be accepted. Initially a 'risk assessment' is carried out, which entails an information gathering exercise :

The women and children should have :

a) Experienced domestic violence – either from a husband, parents, brothers, sisters, in-laws, boyfriends or family.
b) An appropriate number of children can be accommodated (e.g. a woman with 4 children would require 2 rooms, for health and safety reasons, if it's available). Single women are also accepted.
c) Female children of any age, but boys over 12 years of age are not accepted. They can be accommodated with foster carers, arranged by Social Services.
d) No mental health problems, because the refuge does not have 'out of hours' staffing or the professional provision that the woman will require, for example –clinical depression, or suicidal behaviour.
e) No drug or alcohol problems.
f) No medication. Medications need to be monitored and require professional expertise. Women who are on mild anti-depressants are accepted as many of the women are traumatized.
g) They need to be residing outside the refuge area. A woman living locally experiencing domestic violence would not be appropriate for this refuge, for her safety and those of the other residents, as she may be seen by the husband, relations or friends and then followed to the refuge.

Often the risk assessment is done over the phone for expeditiousness.

What the Refuge give the women and children

Once the women and children are accepted, they are given enormous amount of help by the refuge staff, who are there to support the re-organization of their lives and will guide them through the maze of bureaucracy, i.e., solicitors, social security arrangements, maintenance arrangements and application for housing. The first step is – the induction process which entails (Two women support workers in the refuge were interviewed – Gulshan and Zarina):

a) Signing the agreement – it states that the woman abides by the rules and regulations and policies of the refuge.
b) Making her aware of the emergency procedures in the refuge – the 'on-call' system and the panic alarms.
c) Making her aware of the confidentiality issues – if this is breached, the woman and children are asked to leave immediately.
Alternative (mixed) accommodation is provided but not in the refuge. Zarina explains:

Zarina: 'Confidentiality is very, very important because in order for her to be safe here she has to maintain confidentiality of the refuge, the address and everything. No

visitors are allowed, male or female in the refuge, but if there are family and friends that need to pick them up or drop them off, after spending a week-end away, we allow them to find a meeting point, some little distance from the refuge
We do emphasize the fact that they need to let us know if they are going out, if they are staying away for the week-end, we need to know, for health and safety and fire reasons.'

Vital to their needs is protection from harm. Most of the women were terrified of being discovered by their violent husbands. The staff at the refuge provided cover for every weekday from 9am till 5 p.m. Over the night and the week-ends the residents have each other for support and the staff on-call system for emergencies. This alerts the staff on duty to attend the situation. In addition, there are panic alarms that are directly located in the police station, bringing the police to their aid within 2 minutes (the police station was a few doors away). Generally, it is comfortably safe for the women and children as long as they observed the rules of confidentiality.

I asked Zarina what is the initial procedure when the woman has decided to come to the refuge.

Zarina: 'Once we've collected the woman and children, may be from the police station or social services, she might want to buy some things, food etc., but if she has no money then the refuge welfare fund will support her towards the buying of emergency food, for at least ten days.'

On their arrival, to ease the women and children's transition into the refuge, the staff and other residents welcome them with a cooked meal and supportive conversation. Information is given about the town, services, shopping, post-office, schools and local amenities in the area. Once the settling-in time is over, the staff assist the new resident in the procedures of – claiming child benefit, income support, and housing benefit. These processes are essential, as it enables the woman access to funds. Many of the women do not speak, understand or write English and require a good deal of assistance in form filling. Zarina explains about the importance of the paperwork:

Zarina: ' Claiming the women's benefits are very important, our first duties are to get them on income support…if they are already on benefits , the address will need changing. Some women come in with nothing, they've never had any money, they don't even know what (English) money is. If their husbands have been collecting the child benefit then we have to put a new application in.
The women have to pay rent for living here and that comes out of their housing benefit, so we have to fill out the housing benefit forms otherwise we will not get rent…and there will be problems maintaining the refuge.
It will take a week to ten days before benefits are sorted in the meantime, the refuge with their welfare fund will support the women with food etc.'

The staff have a 'link worker' system (not unlike a 'key worker'). Using tailor-made support plans for each resident, the link worker guides them through the work that each resident will require – like, legal help, access to a solicitor (with South Asian language skills), housing, counselling, access to English speaking classes (if required), parenting classes, enrolling children into local schools or nurseries, registration with the local doctor and they will automatically see the health visitor, who visits the refuge weekly. Zarina added:

Zarina: ' Each staff member is a link worker to three or four residents. They have a pack with all the support plans saying how we are going to work with the woman, what support we plan to give them etc. If they are illiterate we have to think about getting them into ...English classes...also parenting skills that they may not have. We get in touch with the 'Family Centre' for that'.
We have good liaison with all the schools in the area...our families are a priority, so the children are admitted more quickly than normal.
Sometimes there are behaviour problems among the children...violence, .aggression towards other children or their mother. We let the health visitor know, who may refer the child on or we have an Asian counsellor, who is multi-lingual, offering six week sessions or more if needed for the woman and child.

Gulshan discusses the outreach service offered by the refuge:

Gulshan : ' ...our services are two-fold – outreach as well as the refuge. We have an outreach worker going out to promote our service....as soon as the women leave the refuge we continue our link with her...that is when the outreach worker comes in...they physically help her to get her things in the car, take her down to the new house, buy things for the house, in a very caring sharing way...our policy does not allow residents back to visit after they've left the refuge.... The outreach staff are willing to help with legal advice, filling in forms...they are visited every now and then - ..they can phone if they need help, we keep links with women who have left 2 -3 years ago.'

There are endless opportunities to discuss any issues with the staff. House meetings are held at regular intervals, where problems pertaining to the refuge are discussed. There is also a cleaning rota, which involves each resident being responsible for defined areas. This is designed to foster an atmosphere of community spirit and solidarity among the residents.

The women and children's experiences

For all of the women, it was their first experience of communal living. Most of them arrived at the refuge in a confused and desperate condition. Their immediate needs are safety, sympathy and an opportunity to talk about their experiences in a secure and non-judgmental atmosphere. There were mixed feelings voiced about their experiences in the refuge, but generally they admitted it was mainly positive. Essentially they all felt safe and protected. They perceived it as a place where everyone derives from a similar ethnic and experiential background. The children were all welcomed by other children in the refuge. The refuge provided space for the children to play together, with specific designated playrooms and a well- appointed walled garden that was child friendly, with an abundance of toys and games to stimulate them. The atmosphere for the children was one of freedom and in many instances this was a first for the child and mother. A recognition of this fact is an important aspect of the healing process for both, mother and children.

Preeya's experience is quite satisfactory, she appreciates the secure environment the refuge offers:

Preeya: :*I am happy that there are other women and children here and that most of all it is safe for us, we would rather be here than anywhere else.'*

L.L.R.: '*Are you able to talk to other women about things? Do you feel comfortable enough to talk about the past?*

Preeya: '*Yes I do – in the evenings we come downstairs to sit and we all talk about our experiences.*

L.L.R.: '*If you could make some changes in the refuge, what would you like to see changed?*

(A number of the women found this question a problem. I'm uncertain if it was the interpretation process or whether they felt that the consequences of giving their opinion would be seen as detrimental. The interpreter – Kal rephrases the question)

Preeya is still not able to answer the question, but instead offers another reply she assumes is suitable. In order to make a change one needs to be in a position to effect the change. Many women in Preeya's situation have never been asked to give their opinion before, therefore the question might be confusing and almost overwhelming. Preeya resorts to an alternative conclusion:

Preeya: '*We were told the rules when we came here and we would not break them or change them, if anybody did they would be out, if any rules were broken, so we would not even consider it...yes, I am quite happy with the rules, if they are broken there would be more pressure on us. We know it's a safe place and we have nowhere else to go,'*

Others like Seema, define the problems:
Seema: '*Here it is difficult...it's very difficult to share with all these women. You have to go by the staff rules, you can't do anything. Because everyone is sharing the bathroom and the kitchen*

and you've got to know who is cooking and when. Sometimes it might be late cooking and it's the same for the bathroom. In our rooms we have a fridge, so we would often cook the food and bring it upstairs and eat. Or maybe wait ages before somebody finishes their cooking and you might wait ages to also use the bathroom. So it has not been easy.,

In Binney, Harkness and Nixon's (1981) study of refuges, many of the women complained about the lack of privacy and bad physical conditions and overcrowding. Nearly half the women shared a bedroom with another family or families as well as their own children, which allowed them no private space for peace and quiet.

The women and children in this study are accommodated in their own rooms, that contain beds for each one, a table and chairs and a built-in wardrobe, a sink with a vanity unit and their own fridge. There were ten bedrooms and four toilets, two laundry rooms, fully equipped with washing machines and tumble dryers, two kitchens two lounges and two playrooms for the children. Clearly an improvement on space and privacy for these women. Another aspect of dissatisfaction in Binney et al.'s study, was the constant noise made by the children (40% mentioned this as a problem).

This was reiterated by Sunita in this study:

Sunita: It's alright but as my room is downstairs, the children in the refuge are forever coming and knocking on my door, if there is nobody around they would come to my door and I'm expected to answer it. My baby does not always get sleep...I am always being disturbed by children playing around.'

Seema felt that the women were not always considerate about the other's needs:

Seema: 'Some of the women don't have children that go to school...I like my daughter in bed at proper times. Some of the ladies don't go to bed till 11p.m. or midnight. They'd be sitting, giggling away or chatting loudly, I'd hear them, I have to get up early for the school run. The next day I'd sometimes hear those ladies complaining about the noise in the morning and they could not sleep and I was talking and disturbing them and the door was banging.'

However, Nina had no complaints:

Nina: 'I'm so pleased I made this decision. I would not go back. When I was there (home) *I was on the go, it seems, 24hours a day. At least here my daughter is happier and settling down. I've got my room and things and as long as all the children are happy it's fine. But if they got into fights and things that would be difficult. Even now the children do have their squabbles...I usually say... to my daughter -."come away, come away with me," There is a baby here in the refuge and my daughter is happy playing with the baby, but she would be happier if she had her brothers here.'* (brothers remained with their father).

Nina expanded on the joys of living in the refuge. She would wake up in the morning and think, how lucky she was to be here, away from harm and suffering.

During the study, I frequently observed a very calm and relaxed atmosphere amongst the women. The children seemed happy to see us (Kal and I), and gathered around to welcome us on our arrival. The younger children played together or stayed close to their mothers while they spoke to us. The children appeared to mix well with each other and often the women take turns in keeping a watch on each other's children, while they cooked or bathed. (This only occurred when the children had been for a longer time at the refuge and would have been comfortable about staying with someone other than their mother, i.e., member of staff or another mother).

The women reported they would spend many evenings in the lounge where they would gather to talk about past or daily events. Often it would centre around their children and their progress. Another activity enjoyed by all the women was watching Bollywood movies. There seemed to be an abundance of videos for them to look at, which they thoroughly enjoyed, bringing romance, humour, drama and escapism into their evenings. This would then become a conversation piece, producing amusing anecdotal flavours.

The length of time the women stayed at the refuge varied. From a few months to two years. On average they would be moved on within eighteen months. Towards the end of a lengthy stay the women often became restless, wanting to move on, tired of communal living and yearning for the independence that has been encouraged throughout their stay. Others were concerned that the long period at the refuge would make it difficult for them to cope on their own, when they do eventually get rehoused. Long-term accommodation was difficult to secure due to housing shortages in the area. This was envisaged to be a growing problem due to a steady flow of asylum seekers and refugees designated to the area.

Complaints about the refuge chiefly focused on practical problems, like accessibility to kitchen and bathroom facilities, with having to take turns at peak times and the occasional noise levels. This was dependent on the ages of the majority of children living in the refuge at any one time. Generally, the women agreed that they had gained from their refuge experience. Mentally and physically they felt stronger and grew in self-confidence. As many of the women and children were kept in enforced isolation by their husbands, the refuge experience enabled them to develop friendships amongst other women and taught them to reorganize and reassess their lives.

Children in the refuge

One of the most striking features of living in a refuge was the need to occupy the children. Previous studies have found that facilities for the children were poor due to lack of space and funding for play equipment. They also found that living with so many children in a confined space was one of the hardest aspects of refuge life (Binney et al. 1981).

At the time of this study, the majority of the children were in the pre-school age group. Only two of the women's children attended school, two attended part-time nursery, one was a baby and one a toddler. Once the women familiarized themselves with the area, many of them would go out together during the day, taking the younger children with them.

The playrooms in the refuge were well stocked with toys and play equipment, but were not always kept open as many of the toys would get broken or lost. The walled garden offered a safe play area for the children. It contained a slide and seating area for adults and children and there was plenty of space for cycling and game activities. Very few of the children needed to be motivated to play in this area, it was safe and child friendly. A covered section provided a shelter for the women and children to gather together on warm evenings.

On their return from school and nursery the children would often play together in the garden, chatting and teasing each other. Most of the children spoke English to each other and Urdu or Punjabi to their mothers. They would proudly show me their artwork and other projects done at school and most appeared to be making good progress in their studies. All enjoyed their new school or nursery and none asked to return to their home or previous schools. Sometimes the children would congregate in Sindy's room to play with her young daughter, who was a favourite. Another favoured activity was playing with Sunita's baby, who was a lovable little boy who was completely adored by all the children there. In fact his socialization skills were highly tuned, he disliked being left for a moment on his own, needing to be in the company of others constantly. Sunita said she would have liked to have seen him able to adjust to some solitary play, but unless asleep, her young baby was happiest when he was getting attention.

Other activities that involved the children were group trips organized by the staff – like shopping trips, going to the cinema, picnics and away-days by the seaside. All of which helped liven the spirits of the women and children to the extent that they felt valued and special.

The refuge did not employ a children's worker, instead the local playgroups and nurseries were used by the children. This encouraged the children to mix and meet other children and gave the women with the school-aged children, some quiet time in the refuge. Debbonaire (1994), describes the invaluable services of the children's support workers that provide specific activities for children in refuges, whose highly skilled work made a positive difference to the children involved. However, it's the usual issues of lack of available funding for children's needs that prevent this service from being a statutory norm.

CHAPTER 8
MOVING ON

Women's refuges can provide salvation for some of the women and children who have been living under the threat of violence.   Often the liminal state of suspension continues for months and sometimes as long as two years or more before they can move on or are re-housed.   This period of reflection on their past lives is an important process for the women, a time for grieving for their various losses endured through violence (Hoff 1990).

The women's experiences can be compared to the continuum of 'rites of passage'. van Genneps's (1990) work on rites of passage emphasizes that society reproduces itself through these rituals.   The person is given a new status without the social structure changing.   According to van Gennep the rites are divided into three phases.   The 'separation', the 'liminal' and the 'reintegration'.   If we apply these stages to the transition processes that the women in the study were undergoing.

We could then say that the 'separation phase', which is characterized by the person moving away from a fixed point towards something unknown, could be the breaking away from the violence and leaving the home.

Once the break is made the person enters the 'liminal phase', a state of limbo, an ambiguous stage where the person is in a sense 'outside' society.   When the woman enters the refuge, she too is in a state of transition.   In traditional societies, 'ritual experts' with community assistance, aid the person/s through such transitions (Turner 1968).   The entire community is normally concerned with the needs and are involved in the transition process of the person/s.   Turner describes this stage as dangerous, as there is a risk that the person/s might reject the change and refuse to be integrated, thereby risks becoming 'socially homeless' or 'invisible'.

A (South) Asian woman leaving her husband is seen as having dishonoured her in-laws and her own family (even if her husband was violent to her). Consequently, she could be left without family or community support, which is exacerbated if she is without any family in England (who might have supported her).   The woman thus takes the risk and moves into this, initially, 'dangerous' but gradually healing phase.   Sometimes the fear of transferring dishonor to the children prevent the woman from leaving.

Finally, the 'reintegration phase', where the person is reinstated, reborn into a new category of social person (Erikson 1995). This, for the woman is the 'moving on' stage, from living in a refuge to being rehoused and being alone with her children. This can be a sharp contrast from the sharing communal life she has become used to, having someone to talk to and feeling safe. The emergence of a new identity.

At the time of the study and during the data analysis stage of the research, three women in the study, had left the refuge. Two were re-housed and one returned to her home, as her husband was now living with his parents. A fourth woman had been asked to leave the refuge because she had breached the rules of confidentiality. This incident developed just prior to the start of the study but due to the woman's refuge involvement, it was decided to include her in the study.

The moving on stage can be an ambiguous time for some. Both Seema and Preeya had been at the refuge for almost two years and both had voiced that they were ready to move on:

Seema: '…my daughter is always asking me, " when are we going to the new house?". I've had to tell her that we will move out of here one day. We've even talked about painting the rooms. My daughter has pictures and poster she wants to put up in the new house'.

Preeya too looked forward to new beginnings:

Preeya: 'We hopefully want to get a place of our own soon. My daughter would be in full time school and after settling in a bit I could look for a job'.

Both Preeya and Seema are now in their own homes.
Preeya got a new house on a recently built development not far from the refuge and has settled down well with her daughter. She says that she has not thought of getting married again, but would like to visit her parents in India sometime. She does not want to settle down in India, as her husband has contact arrangements with her daughter and there may be problems taking her out of the country.

Seema too was anxious to be re-housed. During the latter part of this study, Seema and her daughter were offered accommodation in the area. When she went to view it, she was very distressed, feeling insecure and unsafe in the property. The windows were the problem, she says. They were too large and she felt frightened and vulnerable. She was fortunate to be offered alternative accommodation which she then accepted. A few days prior to her moving, she became tearful and had to be reassured. Because she was threatened by her husband when she left him, she was frequently in fear of seeing him again. It was for this reason and the violence towards her daughter, that contact with him was not recommended. Seema was not located very close to the refuge and hence would have to begin to acquaint herself with her new neighbourhood. It was a combination of all these facts and the issue of being on her own with her daughter for the first time that was worrying Seema.

Neelam and her son returned to their own home after her husband went to live with his parents. Social services will continue to follow up her case, to ensure that for the present time, her husband does not have contact with her son. Her son's behaviour has improved, since his arrival at the refuge. He will be monitored by the professionals for a while yet.

Nina and her daughter will remain in the refuge. She says she needs time with other people and time to adjust to her new found freedom. Nina has accomplished a great deal in terms of her self-development. She says she has emerged stronger and has a whole new life to look forward to. Her daughter attends nursery and will have a school placement in the new year. Both continue to thrive in the company of the refuge residents.

Nina has recently told me about the contact arrangements with her sons. She has seen them on two occasions in the company of their father and supervised by a social worker. They seemed happy to see their mother and sister again. On the second visit, they remained in close proximity to their father. Nina reports that they might have been warned against going near her and getting too friendly. She said her husband was scornful of her healthy appearance and tried to erode her confidence by snide remarks. She was undeterred and remained calm.

Sunita had a few 'access to benefits' problems. The refuge staff are endeavouring to resolve them for her. Her immigrant status is also in question and for this a solicitor has been appointed to guide her through. Her baby continues to be the main attraction at the refuge, with no obvious difficulties envisaged. She is optimistic about the future as long as she is allowed to remain in the U.K. In India she would receive unequal status as a divorcee.

Sindy and her daughter will remain at the refuge for a little longer. There are no imminent plans for them to be re-housed. Sindy has moved on in terms of her confidence and self-esteem and is positive about the future for herself and her daughter.

Tina remains in the homeless hostel. She missed the camaraderie spirit of the refuge, when she moved out but continues to keep in contact with ther friends there. With her sewing skills, she often takes orders to make up the women's *salwha kahmeese* (long sleeved tunic with loose fitting trousers, traditionally worn by women in India and Pakistan). To celebrate her daughter's fifth birthday, Tina threw a small party at the hostel, inviting all the refuge staff and residents and ourselves. All the food was prepared and cooked by Tina and the women at the refuge.   Now that her daughter had started school, Tina has expressed that she does not look forward to spending the days on her own, in fact she wonders how she will cope being alone in the future.   She will not consider marrying again because she already has her husband's child and she feels that her daughter would not get the love that her real father would have given her.

CHAPTER 9
CONCLUSION

This study uncovered the particular difficulties faced by traditional South Asian women in Britain who have suffered domestic violence. It looked at the experiences of these women and their children in the aftermath of the violence and within the context of a specific South Asian women's refuge. It was a small scale study centered around seven women and their children and although the research highlighted specific cultural difficulties, it was not possible to generalize from a sample of this size. However, many important issues were raised and so some conclusions can be reached.

The study was not without constraints. The insufficiency of anthropological literature on domestic violence is particularly noted. Although anthropologists have, in recent times, moved away from small scale rural non-Western societies, to more urban industrialized settings and migrant communities, it has nonetheless refrained from the more darker issues of familial violence within groups. Shaw's (2000) account of Pakistani migration to Britain and their settlement in Oxford originated from an assimilationist argument. She discusses controversial topics like caste and Islamic sect, in an objective and accurate manner, but does not report on any domestic violence issues or indeed the attitudes to the phenomena.

Domestic violence identified in all its forms by the women's experiences in this study was quite alarming. Their community norms and traditional values masked the suffering of the women and children, portraying a picture of marital harmony and cultural cohesion. Under the respect for privacy, the abuse and torture of women by their husbands and their families was allowed to go on, silently. Some of the children were caught up in the process and consequently received a share of the abuse.

Previous studies have indicated that the impact of domestic violence can have detrimental effects on children (Hester et al, 2000, Kelly 1994) In this study the source of the data were the mothers, who reported on their children's experiences. Apart from the baby, the impact of the experience of domestic violence on the remaining children varied enormously. Much of the evidence reinforces the findings of Hester et al. As the children have now been removed from the context of violence, the repercussions of the trauma may be experienced by a wide range of behavioural, physical and psychological effects, long and short term. Some of the mothers reported nightmares and children's anxieties triggered by visual and verbal suggestions. It was noted that none of the mothers talked to their children about the violence, whether they were frightened, missed their home, etc. Generally, they were unsure of the consequences and all agreed that it was unfruitful to discuss, using secrecy as a protective strategy. Neither did the children spontaneously discuss issues with their mother, nor were they given opportunities to do so. McGee (forthcoming), suggested that children generally want to talk about their experiences of domestic violence. During a play session in this study, it was difficult to engage two of the children and it was felt that the sessions needed further development and the expertise of a play or art therapist and was hence, not included in the research findings.

All the women in the study wanted their marriage to succeed and some were willing to endure adulterous husbands for his family's support. In all cases, it was evident that their interests were secondary to those of everyone else around. The marriages were all arranged for the women, leaving them little or no choice. Apart from one woman whose family approached a marriage bureau on her behalf, allowing her some choice. Many of the women's families believed that their daughter's future was secured abroad and had no knowledge or indeed, some were misled by the spouse's true circumstances in Britain. This allowed their daughters to be placed in a particularly vulnerable position when the marriage ran into difficulties.

Language (or the lack of speaking English) was a huge problem for all the women in the study. This effectively isolated them and lessened their opportunities for accessing outside agencies and offered the abuser/s a greater degree of control and power to continue the oppression. Many of these women were oblivious of their rights and entitlements and were allowed to be kept that way.

The majority of the women were dependent wives and were less empowered to challenge or resist violence, however, the wives who had some supposedly *'economic autonomy'* were equally impoverished and deprived and subjected to abuse, making it clear that earning an income did not amount to power or equality in women's relationship with men (Mama 1989).

The *'one year'* (then 2 year) immigration rule designed to prevent people from abusing the system for entering Britain, clearly disadvantages women suffering from domestic violence. With the threat of deportation, the woman declines from reporting the violence. Additionally, there is the fear of being returned to her country of origin in disgrace and shame, coupled with the fact that she would probably have to leave her children (child) behind in Britain. None of the women interviewed in this study were knowledgeable about this issue, most of their passports were kept by their husbands who used these various forms of oppression to increase and exercise their power over their wives.

It is clear from this research that there are many issues of concern that exist.

a) A fuller understanding of the problems by the relevant agencies
b) An improved access to services that provide interpreters should be mandatory in areas with large ethnic populations.
c) Further education and training of the agencies involved (housing, social service, police and other health professionals).
d) Comprehension of the degree and extent of this particular violence should be mandatory in the training of all the above service providers.
e) Evaluation on how present services respond to black and ethnic minority women's needs would be useful and would go towards (hopefully) further improvements.
f) Further research is required into ethnic minority children's perceptions and reactions to living with domestic violence, they should be allowed to define the impact of their experiences.
g) Therapy and counselling services specifically for children and women who have suffered domestic violence, especially tailored to accommodate language and culture.
h) There is a need for more refuges in urban areas with high populations of black and ethnic minority populations (BME), catering for the specific cultural needs, as accommodating women and children from these groups within a generic refuge will further exacerbate their already complex and specific needs.

Finally, this ethnography grew out of a need to investigate the existence and the nature of the phenomena of domestic violence amongst a group of South Asian women and their children living in a refuge. Through their narratives, I aimed to interpret their experiences. However, what it means to interpret and what it means to experience are two highly relative contextual concepts, as Clifford Geertz (1983) observed. He recommended that we familiarized ourselves to *"local knowledges"* and refrain from the futility of describing a universalized human social world. The experiences narrated in this ethnographic fieldwork are human experiences that are individualized and contextualized against a background of differing forms of violence, cultural values and traditional and family obligations.

Additional note:

In 2015 the women's refuge in the study was closed down by the local council due to financial restraints. The women and children were relocated to other mainly generic refuges. Many problems were reported by these women in the generic refuges that do not cater to the needs of these specific groups of women and children. For example – the women and children found themselves in the taboo environment of smoking. Also, certain foods like pork and beef which are forbidden due to religious beliefs, were sometimes offered to the children in the generic refuges.

These issues have forced some women to seek refuge elsewhere with relatives, but due to its dangers of disclosure, they are compelled to move frequently therefore signaling hazards for (South) Asian women, that leaving home or speaking out entails losing both sides of their families.

EPILOGUE

The Current Legal Situation

- **December 2009** – The Home Office launched a pilot project – the 'Sojourner Project' to assist victims of domestic violence with No Recourse to Public Funds (NRPF)
- **July 2010** – Home Secretary – Theresa May announced that the 'Sojourner Project' will continue till March 2012 pending a longer term solution. The women with NRPF and immigration problems will have access to housing and subsistence costs for up to 40 days for those who apply to remain in the UK under the 'Domestic Violence Rule' and will be extended to March 2011.
- **April 2012** – Home Office announced an action plan to provide training to community and women's organizations across UK to enable support of women's access to the 'Sojourner Project' scheme and other services to address immigration and NRPF problems.
- **March 2016** – Home Office 2016 – 20 strategy to end violence to women includes £80 million of dedicated funding to provide core-support for refuges and other accommodation based services, rape support centres, and national helplines.
- **From April 2017** - A new 'Violence Against Women & Girls Service Transformation Fund - will support local and domestic service provision.
- **SEWAK** – Is a Black and Ethnic Minority (BME) refuge that is currently seeking to replace the refuge in the study.
  info@sewakhousingservicesltd.org.uk

BIBLIOGRAPHY

AHMED, S. (1986) *'Cultural Racism in work with Asian women & Girls'* in **Ahmed, S., Cheetham, J., & Small, J. (eds)** 'Social Work with Black children & their families' London: Batsford.

AHMED, S. (1992) 'Women & Gender in Islam' Newhaven & London: Yale University Press.

BALLARD, R. & BALLARD, C. (1977) *'The Sikhs: The development of South Asian settlements in Britain'* in **Watson, J.L. (ed)** 'Between Two Cultures: Migrants & Minorities in Britain' Oxford Basil Blackwell.

BHATTI-SINCLAIR, K. (1994) *'Asian Women & Violence from Male Partners'* in **Lupton, C. & Gillespie, T. (eds)** 'Working with Violence' Basingstoke: Macmillian Press.

BINNEY, V., HARKNELL, G. & NIXON, J. (1981) 'Leaving Violent Men: A study of Refuges & Housing for Battered Women' Leeds: Women's Aid Federation. England.

BOWSTEAD, J., LALL, D. & RASHID, J. (1995) 'Asian Women & Domestic Violence – Information for Advisors' London: London Borough of Greenwich Women's Equality Unit.

CAROLL, L. (1998) 'Arranged Marriages: Law, Customs & the Muslim girl in the U.K.' Women living under Muslim laws. Dossier (20)

CHOUDRY, S. (1996) 'Pakistani Women's Experiences of Domestic Violence in Great Britain' Home Office Research Studies RF43 London.

DAVIS, S. (1994) 'Women & Violence – Realities & Responses Worldwide' Zed Books. London.

DEBBONAIRE, T. (1994) *'Work with Children in Women's Aid Refuges & After'* in **Mullender, a & Morley, R. (eds)** 'Children living with Domestic Violence: Putting men's abuse of women on the child care agenda'. Whiting & Birch Ltd. London.

DONNAN, H. (1985) *'The Rules & the Rhetoric of Marriage negotiations among the Dhund Abbasi of North East Pakistan'* in **Shaw, A.** 'Kinship & Continuity: Pakistani families in Britain'. Gorden & Breech Pubs.

ERIKSEN, T.H. (1995) 'Small Places, Large Issues – An introduction to Social & Cultural Anthropology'. Pluto Press. London.

EVASON, E. (1982) 'Hidden Violence: A study of Battered Women in Northern Ireland'. Belfast: Farset Press.

FANTUZZO, J.W. & LINQUIST, C.U. (1989) 'The effects of observing conjugal violence on children: A review & analysis of research methodology'. *Journal of Family Violence 4 (1) 77-94.*

GEERTZ, C. (1983) 'Local Knowledge: Further essays in interpretive anthropology'. New York: Basic Books

GILLESPIE, G. (1995) 'Television, Ethnicity & Cultural Change'. London & New York. Routledge.

HAGUE, G. & MALOS, E. (1993) 'Domestic Violence – Action for Change'. Cheltenham: New Clarion Press.

HAGUE, G., KELLY, L., MALOS, R. & MULLEMDER, A. (1996) 'Children, Domestic Violence & Refuges: A Study of Needs & Responses' Bristol: Women's Aid Federation (England)

HALLETT, C. (1995) *'Child Abuse: An Academic Overview'* in **Kingston, P. & Penhale, B. (eds)** 'Family Violence & the Caring Professions'. Basingstoke: Macmillan.

HELLMAN, C.G. (2001) 'Culture, Health & Illness'. Arnold Publishers. London.

HESTER, M. & RADFORD, L. (1992) *'Domestic Violence & Access Arrangements for Children in Denmark & Britain'* in **Hester, M., Pearson, C. & Harwin, N.** 'Making an Impact – Children & Domestic Violence'. Jessica Kingsley Publishers Ltd. London.

HESTER, M., PEARSON, C. & HARWIN, N. (2000) 'Making an Impact – Children & Domestic Violence'. Jessica Kingsley Publishers. London.

HOFF, L. (1990) 'Battered Women as Survivors'. London : Routledge.

HOLDEN, G.W. & RITCHIE, K.L. (1991) ''Linking extreme marital discord, child rearing & child behaviour problems: Evidence from Battered Women' *Child Development 62, 311 -327.*

HOME OFFICE AFFAIRS COMMITTEE (1993) ' Home Affairs Committee on Domestic Violence' pp. 78 – 79, Table 4.4. London H.M.S.O.

HUGHES, H.M. (1988) *Psychological & Behavioural Correlates of Family Violence in Child Witnesses & Victims'* in **Hester, M., Pearson, C. & Harwin, N.** 'Making an Impact – Children & Domestic Violence'. Jessica Kingsley Publishers. London.

IMAM, U.F. (1994) *'Asian Children & Domestic Violence'* in **Mullender, a. & Morley, R. (eds)** 'Children living with Domestic Violence – Putting Men's abuse of Women on the Child Care Agenda'. Whiting & Birch. London.

KELLY, L. (1988) 'Surviving Sexual Violence'. Cambridge : Polity Press.

KELLY, L. (1994) *The Interconnectedness of Domestic Violence & Child Abuse: Challenges for Research, Policy & Practice'* in **Mullender, A. & Morley, R.** 'Children living with Domestic Violence – Putting Men's abuse of Women on the Child Care Agenda'. Whiting & Birch. London.

KELLY, L. & RADFORD, J. (1996) *Nothing really happened: The invalidation of Women's experiences of sexual violence'* in **Hester, M., Kelly, L. & Radford, J. (eds)** 'Women, Violence & Male Power'. Open University Press.

MAMA, A. (1989) 'The Hidden Struggle' London: London Race &

McGEE, C. (Forthcoming) *'Children's & Mother's Experiences of Child Protection following Domestic Violence'* in **Hester, M., Pearson, C. & Harwin, N.** 'Making an Impact – Children & Domestic Violence'. Jessica Kingsley Publishers. London.

MOORE, J.G. (1975) 'Yo-Yo Children – Victims of Matrimonial Violence' *Child Welfare* **54** *(8) 557 – 566*

MULLENDER, A. & MORLEY, R. (1994) 'Children living with Domestic Violence – putting men's abuse of children on the Child Care Agenda'. Whiting & Birch. London.

ORTNER, S.B. (1974) *'Is Female to Male as Nature is to Culture?'* in **Rosaldo, M. & Lamphere, L. (eds)** 'Women, Culture & Society'. Stanford, C.A. : Stanford University Press.

PHAL, J. (ed) (1985) 'Private Violence & Public Policy'. London: Routledge.

SHAW, A. (2000) 'Kinship & Continuity : Pakistani Families in Britain'. Gorden & Breech Publishing Group.

SMITH, L. (1989) 'Domestic Violence : An Overview of the Literature'. Home Office Research Studies. 107. London H.M.S.O.

STAGG, V., WILLS, G.D. & HOWELL, M. (1989) 'Psychopathology in early childhood witnesses of family violence'. *Topics in early Childhood Education* **9** 73 – 87.**TAYLOR, J.H.** (1976) 'The Halfway Generation: A study of Asian Youths in Newcastle-upon-Tyne'. Windsor. NFER Publishing

TURNER, V. (1968) *'The Science of Culture'* in **Morten Fried (ed)** 'Readings in Anthropology' *Cultural Anthropology* **Vol II.** New York. Crowell.

UDDIN, B. & AHMED, L. (2000) 'A choice by right: The report of the Working Group on Forced Marriage'. London. Home Office. Communication Directorate.

UNITED NATIONS RESOURCE MANUEL (June 1993) ' *Strategies for confronting Domestic Violence'* in **Davies, M. (ed)** 'Women & Violence – Realities & Responses Worldwide'. Zed Books Ltd. London.

VAN GENNEP, A. (1909) *'Les Rites de Passage'* in **Erikson, T.H.** 'Small Places, Large Issues – An Introduction to Social & Cultural Anthropology'. Pluto Press.

WESTRA, B. & MARTIN, H.P. (1981) 'Children of Battered Women'. *Maternal-Child Nursing Journal.* Spring **10** (1) pp.41 – 54.

WOMEN'S AID (2015 – Survey)

ABOUT THE AUTHOR

The author was born in Bombay (now Mumbai) is of Anglo-Indian parentage and spent her childhood in India. She was educated in Bombay and England. This study is part of her MSc in Social Anthropology at the Brunel University, London, U.K., conducted in 2002. During the time of this study the author was a practicing health visitor in the local community and the health professional overseeing the (South) Asian women's refuge depicted in the study. She has three children and lives in England, U.K.

(Front cover illustration – *Repetitious Afflictions of 'Love'* by Donna-Louise Richardson)